Dew Yew Keep a' Troshin!

OLD BARNEY'S BROADCASTS

VOLUME ONE

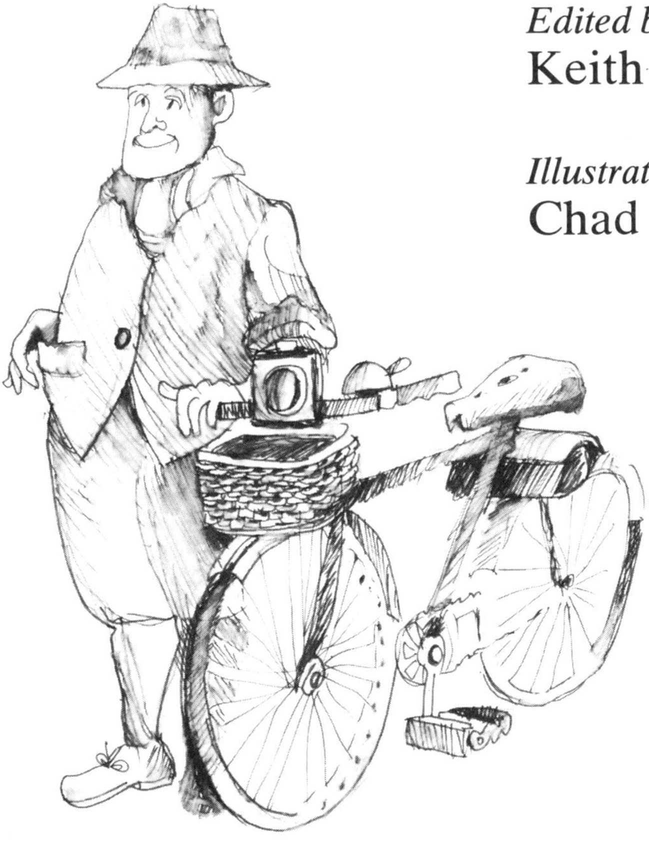

Edited by
Keith Skipper

Illustrated by
Chad

JPB

Typeset by Fakenham Photosetting Ltd.
Reproduced by Colourplan and Printed by
Colourprint
Bound by Dickens Print Trade Finishers

A Product of Fakenham

FOREWORD

Old Barney gets about. He's known and loved by those lucky enough to come within earshot. Now the words are being recorded for posterity.

Since coming to live in Norfolk, I've often been accused of talking a lot of "Old Blarney". Believe me, I've done my best to talk more like Old Barney so that my utterances might be more easily understood.

I'm still floundering with every effort to get to grips with the Norfolk accent . . . but this magnificent book provides timely inspiration!

Long may accents and dialects reign. We have several in my own country, some of which I can master to a reasonable extent, while others are quite beyond me.

I've noticed several pronounced similarities between the way we speak in Ireland and the way the Norfolk dialect is used. It's not just the way that people talk; it reflects also the way they think.

When I first came here, I was amazed at the amount of common ground between Ireland and Norfolk. For example, the clothes, and the gait which comes of walking over arable land, are common to both.

I've been here long enough to know the Norfolk dialect is precious, and will remain a significant emblem of pride for all those born in this Royal county.

All the world's a stage, and there is no reason why a true Norfolk man cannot have his place on it. May Old Barney keep a' troshin for many a long day to come.

Dick Condon,
Theatre Royal,
Norwich.

INTRODUCTION

Keith Skipper

He'll hate me for saying it, but Old Barney is a modern media star. Where other outstanding Norfolk characters before him had to rely largely on local publications, and personal appearances, to propagate their philosophies, he has found his niche in front of a microphone.

Reluctant at first to enter the technological arena, BBC Radio Norfolk's rural correspondent has accepted the un-doubted value of using the airwaves to reach a regular audi-ence of thousands on Saturday mornings.

In fact, he and his devoted listeners had to come to terms with the vagaries of radio programme rescheduling ... Old Barney's spot was round about midday from his arrival in September, 1980, until early October, 1983. Then changes at Norfolk Tower signalled a new time for rustic ramblings at 8.30 on a Saturday morning. Fortunately, Old Barney has been able to meet fresh demands, although the journey into Norwich on his trusty old bike can prove hazardous in bad weather, or after a heavy night at his beloved Datty Duck, the village pub which inspires so much of his material.

He's more an observer of others than a character anxious to talk about himself. We know he's retired after working on the land. He's a bachelor and has lived in the same village all his life. He has strong views on the way the Norfolk countryside is changing, and is always ready to say his piece on this and other topics. But he retains an air of mystery when it comes to other personal details.

Old Barney may well be right in claiming this should not detract from the truth and value of what he says, and his pride in championing the local dialect is hardly open to question.

He refuses to open garden fetes or give after-dinner speeches. He's not after that kind of adulation or attention, preferring the comparative anonymity the wireless studio affords. Eventually, he allowed me to become a sort of Boswell to his Dr. Johnson, although the only biographical details you'll find are in his own words.

Clearly, there are no hard and fast rules in writing down the vernacular as, indeed, there are no guarantees that a particular phrase or saying commonly used in the Datty Duck is employed in all parts of Norfolk.

Different villages, even different families, have their own ways of expressing themselves, and I suspect Old Barney and his rural colleagues have over the years built up a vocabulary bank on which they can draw for their own amusement or, on occasions, to confuse the "furriners".

As far as possible, I've remained true to his original broadcasts, with the help of his scribbled notes and verbal guidance. As he points out, these are his spoken words, laced with Norfolk humour and expressions – many of them highly individual – and they stand up best, I think, when read out loud. Those with a genuine feel for Norfolk dialect should manage that without much trouble.

Newcomers anxious to catch the right flavour might be glad of a few tips on phonetics, although I stress this book is essentially for amusement rather than an analytical guide through the dialect jungle. Old Barney's catchphrase "Dew yew keep a' troshin!" is simply an encouragement to keep at it, to do your own thing. In America, they'd probably say "Keep on truckin'!".

"Troshin" is a corruption of threshing, and sorting out the wheat from the chaff is a sound occupation for all clear-thinking people.

Running two or three words into each other is regular practice. A few examples: "I suppose" becomes "spooz" – "going to" is "gorter" or "gorta" – "a bit of" is shortened to "bitter" – "some of them" becomes "sum onnem" and "come out of" is transformed into "cumowter" – "must have retired" turns into "muster retyred" and "in front of" is abbreviated into "frutter". Many words beginning with the letter "v" are given a "w" start instead, like "willuj" for "village" and "wikker" for "vicar". Old Barney's highly individual style is emphasised in lines like "Dunt yew paggarter orl his skwit!''. A clinical translation provides ''Don't pay any regard to all his nonsense''. I leave it to you to decide which is the more colourful. He also invents a lot of his own words and phrases, but most of them are easy to follow in the context of what he's talking about.

''Coronearshun milk'' comes out of a tin. ''HelterSkeltzer'' fizzes in the glass. ''The defective van'' checks if you have a television licence.

There are obvious discrepancies in style. ''Going to ask'' is ''gorta arsk'' on some occasions, and ''gorter arsk'' on others, while ''go to France'' comes out as ''go ter Frarnse''. For the sake of uniformity, I could have tightened up in these specific areas, but I think the old boy's variations add spice to the rural mixture. This collection respresents only the start of Old Barney's broadcasting career, from September 13th, 1980, to February 14th, 1981 – two dozen contributions in chronological order. Of course, there are plenty more where they come from. He's been in full cry since BBC Radio Norfolk opened, and we hope this is the first volume of many dedicated to the unfading delights of our local dialect. My warmest thanks to Chad for his splendid illustrations. Perhaps he's better known as a pub entertainer, with guitar and quips at the ready, but his talents as an artist are given full rein as he puts Old Barney and his village colleagues on parade. No doubt, Chad's familiarity with the local pub scene helped him come to terms quickly with the admirable decor of the Datty Duck!

Thanks also to Dick Condon for his friendly foreword. I know our rural correspondent is highly flattered by such kind words from 'Old Blarney' – and both are doing so much to keep culture thriving in Norfolk. Dick retains a natural affection for his native brogue, but he has noticed clear similarities between our basic philosophies and those of the Emerald Isle. And whether you're filling a theatre or emptying a pint pot, the text is the same ... Dew yew keep a' troshin!

◇ *OLD BARNEY ARRIVES* ◇

Broadcast just before midday on Saturday, September 13th, 1980, two days after the official opening of BBC Radio Norfolk. The appeal for a regular rural correspondent is answered immediately by this son of the soil. Old Barney makes it clear how he sees his role in the media, and reveals many of his uncompromising rustic philosophies.

Mornin' ter orl on yer. Spooz fast thing yewre gorta arsk is how a country bor lyke me kin git his own little spot on thole wireless. Well, I kin arnser that wun pritty sharpish. This heer lot on Reardyo Norfik watted sumwun wi' thar lug ter the grownd deep in th' harter the country, and yew hatta be up fearly arly in the mornin' ter catch me owt when that cum ter raral 'fairs.

Ire bin cloos ter the soyl orl my loife, an I rekun I know b' now wot mearke us tick owt heer. We dew hoss itter Norridge now an' gin ter dew a bitter shoppin an garp rown the market, but thass allus nyce ter git hoom, put yer ole feet up an git the kittle on.

Summer them yung 'uns, speshlly them bitser mawthers orl dolled up wi' thar oiy shadder an' that, they ent satisfyed wi' a nite down the pub or a bitter skwit at the willuj darnse. They cleer orf ter them diskothews ter git deffened an' gollop rown in thar fansy clobba. Oi arnter nockin' onnem. Theyre gotta spend thar munny on suffin, I spooz, but yew dunt go a lot on that sorta thing if yewre bin up sinse afore six in the mornin', a' milkin' thole cows and then gittin the harvest in. Now I'yre retyred lyke, I dew hev a bitter tyme ter hop on m' byke an' corl on summer my ole meartes. We wuzzer clackin' thuther day bowt harvests o' yeers ago when we fast started wak. Orl them bewtiful hosses an' luvvly little boinders ... that wuz whooly qwyet longside thees heer combynes an' driers they hev terday.

Thass rearl poynt, yer know, we got the job dun jest the searme, even if that did tearke bit longer. Summer them fewls wot chearse bowt till they jest bowt meet tharselves a' cummin' back, orl they finish up with is a koronary. I'yre sin sum on' em beltin trew the willuj orf the mearn rood in thar smart new Cerpryse. Hent gotta minnet ter live, moost onnem – an' they dunt zakkly tearke root in the pub if they dew fynd tyme ter drop in fer a harf. Oonly tyme they say "Are yer gorta hev wun?" is when theyre bloomin' lorst! An' yit, theyre the wuns wot tearke the jews owter us, an' say weer ahynd the tymes an' livin in the parst. Praps we dunt hoss 'long lyke that Steve Ovett – heel bust a gut afore heer dun – an' we sartanly dunt git ahynd rest o' orl them cars on Bank Hollerdays, or go ter Frarnse an' hoop we kin git gack b' Chrismuss!

Yeh, we dew tearke 't bit moor eezy, thass why yew see ser menny ole boys lookin' sharp an' fuller beenz down the Datty Duck. They tearke it eezy, speshlly when thass thar tann ter gitter rownd in. We did berry ole Jearcub Stearnes larst Thassday. But that wunt much orrer sprize rearly. He wuz ded. So, dunt fergit . . . that ent them wot go the kwickest wot git things dun the best. Yewre gotta hev tyme fer a larf anner bitter yap, hent yer? Thass bin my motto sinse I fast wenter muckspreadin' longa ole Horry Mason. "No need ter go barmy, bor" he say ter me. "Yewre gotta hev a bitter enjy left ter lift that pynt Oim gorta buy yer." He nivver did, but that larnt me good lessun orl the searme.

Oill hev nuvver little yarn wiyyer next week. Thankyer muther fer the rabbit. Mynd how yer go, and dunt yew fergit yew lot. Dew yew keep a' troshin!

Old Barney's second broadcast on Saturday, September 20th, 1980, suggests he's already become a bit of a celebrity in his own village, and he introduces some of the characters who frequent the local pub, The Datty Duck. Gibby Painter steps into the sporting spotlight – and shows why he's hardly a favourite with the darts team.

Mornin' ter orl on yer. Well, I hent had nunner that theer fan mearl arter m' bit larst Satterday, but wun or tewer the lokals hev bin a bit moor perlite thun ewsual. Poostman say he hent hard noffin lyke it in orl his natewral, whyle Billa Jarmany rekun he nearla chooked on his meddsun when my voyce cumowter his old wireless.

"Cor, blarst me, that wuz whooly a 'rummin' ter heer yew a' yappin' and I coont see yer. Yewll be on the flippin' telly next longer that Tarry Wergan blook. He kin dew a progrum on yar brayne ... an' corl it 'Blankity Blank!'" – Ole Billa started corffin an' spittin', and I thowt he wuz a gorta brearke in harf, but he cum rownd in tyme ter git down the pub an' weart fer sumwun else ter bung fer a pynt. He ent as sorft as he look, even if he hev gotta bitter bronikul trubble.

Well, thole harvest is jest bowt cleered up. They ewsed ter say, "Orl is searfley gathered in. Sum is troshed an' gonter Lynn!" Good ole bitter skwit, but as I wuz a' sayin' larst week, harvests arnt wot they ewsed ter be. They hent harf chearnjed longer the tearster yer beer. An ent that a bloomin' pryce theez days! Yew carnt ford ter go owt an' git't down onyer lyke yer ewsed tew. I rekun a good skulleark corst a kwid or tew, and thenyer hatta fynd few bob fer that stuff wot fizz in the glarss ... yew know, that HelterSkeltzer. That mearke me feel orl funny lyke till I git next mugger beer in m' hands.

Inflearshun cort up wi' us anorl owt heer in the country, an'

He watted ter kill fifty tew . . . but three savanteens dint leave him a lot ter go for. They rekun Gibby gotta free transfer arter that little lot.

theyre even got wunner them speers vearders down Datty Duck. Carnt wak flippin' thing owt mesself, but that Jeremy Spindlehurst's a rite proppa show orff, flickin' heer an' pushin' theer. Them mawthers think heez suffin speshul wi' them smart sewts an a' buyin' onnem woddkers an' blackcurrents. Now he IS as sorft as he dew look, and they hatta tann him down fer the darts teem cors he coont howld his beer.

They hev sum ryte ole dews, an thass no good a' bein harf cut for they start. They oonly lorst cuppeler gearmes in summer Leeg, an that wuz cors Gibby Painter coont add up proppa.

He watted thatty-eart ter finish ginst Dorg an' Partridje. Arter hossin' fast dart itter dubbel twalve, he wuz ser bloomin' noyyed he chucked uther tew otter floor. Theer wuz a rite ole barney, I kinn tellyer, and he dint git ner hot spuds that nite.

He mearde his cumback ginst Royal Ook arter cuppel weeks suspenshun, an' blarst if he dint tiddel't up agin! Gibby storked upter the bord fuller hisself when he watted ter kill fifty tew. He had sum fansy idears bowt tribbles an' at, but three savanteens dint leave him a lot ter go for. Ole captun went fer him suffin' wicket, an' they rekun Gibby gotta free transfar arter that little lot.

I dunt play ner more mesself. Orl this aggrevearshun an' tenshun ... that cnt wath it. I let 'em git on wi' it, thow I dew scoor cearshanlly when Cloddy Gates fergit his calculearter.

Well, Ire gotter git onter the gardin this arternewn, an' clear owt thole shud. Oill hev nuther littel natter wiyyer next week. Mynd how yer go, add up proppa if yer playin' darts, shewt streart. And dunt yew fergit yew lot. Thassit ... Dew yew keep a' troshin!

*We started a' larfin as the sorft tewl waggled his owld hips, and then
sum brite spark started a' singin: "Heyya gotta lite meter, boy!"*

◇ *CLODDY'S CALCULATOR* ◇

Old Barney's closest friend and confindant is Cloddy Gates. They share many adventures, although both are reluctant to leave the confines of the village. Cloddy's amorous escapades are in the future. In his broadcast of September 27th, 1980, Old Barney recalls another memorable sporting incident in which Cloddy plays a leading part.

Mornin' ter orl on yer. I wuzzer tellin on yer larst week bowt Cloddy Gates. He hev got wunner them thar calculearters wot he bring ter the darts match when he dunt fergit it. We arnt tew sartan if he kin actewlly cownt proppa, but we dunt paggarter orl his skwit. Jest cors he allus wear them ole overawls and ole stror hat wi' a hool innit dunt meen he ent orl theer. I rekun parsunlly heez bit briter than he let on.

Yew jest tearke way he sorted owt rum ole dew in larst cricket match o' season when marryed took on singled blooks. Cloddy greed ter' umpyre longas they bunged fer his beer arterwords. Bilko Butterfield wuz spoozed ter be at thuther ind, an' we rekun he muster hed his jews itter him for the gearme way he kept hossin over the hidje an' upsettin' the cow tads. They cont entertearn him fer leeg fixtyers on Satterdays cors pubs ent cloosed on tyme.

Gittin' back ter this heer gearme atwin the marryed and the singled. That wuzzer gowin orrite until arter tea when sum onnem hatta clear orff an' dew the milkin'. They wunt low ner subsitewts, so Passy Grimshaw's lot hatta bat wi' six men, an' they still watted thatty-foyve ter win when larst cuppel cum tergether. Cloddy wuz honist nuff ter say he wunter lookin' when hollers went up for a stumpin', but he hent got'n' arnser when the batsmin pealed ginst the lite. He hedda wad longer Bilko Butterfield, who say that wuz dark nuff ter go orff ter the pub, but that did pear ter moost on us wotchin' there wunt ner reason fer corlin' itter day. Theer wuz lotter argrin the toss, an' bitter comoshun when the wimmun wot had dun the tees started clackin' an' tellin' each uther ter howld thar slarver. Chap from the brarry wot had cum ter present the troofy say he dint want ner moor sandwidges an' cleered orff.

Cloddy towld em orl ter shut up, an' then he stuck his hand itter pockit o' his ole white coot. "Ire gotta lite meter heer!" he say.

"Lyke wot that Dicky Badd ewse in the Test Match. Howld yew hard whyle I tearke fishal readin'". He held it lorft orl seryus, an' went upandown the pitch lyke wunner them fansy mawthers wot prarnse bowt in the boxin' ring wi' number on a card atwin rownds. ... We started a' larfin as the sorft tewl waggled his owld hips, an then sum brite spark started a' singin' "Heyya gotta lite meter, boy!"

Wuh, that did it. Thole wimmun cum owtfer a garp an' fell bowt larfin'. Them wot wuz spoozed ter be a' playin', they lyned up ahind Cloddy, an' didder sorta conger back ter thole shud where they chearnje. That wuz pritta dark b' now, so nowun cumplearned when Bilko Butterfield nownced Datty Duck wuz opin. I went down longer Cloddy ... an' he gimme a wink when he took his calculearter owter his pocket an' held that up ter the sky.

"Yew crarfty ole sod!" I say ter him. "Keep yew qwyet, ole partner, an' Oill bung fer a pynt," he say. He didanorl. I hatta smyle when they arsked Cloddy ter scoor fer darts, an' he say he hent got his calculearter longer him. He wunt shorter noffin else thow, wuz he? Thass no good a' gittin' owld less yer screw yer biskit. ...

Oill hev nuther little yarn wiyyer next week. Mynd how yer go. Dunt git cort owt if yer dew bitter umpyrin. And dunt yew fergit, yew lot ... Dew yew keep a' troshin!

◇ *THE HARVEST SUPPER* ◇

The village get-together is a traditional part of rural life, whatever the time of year. Old Barney's mardle on Saturday, October 4th, 1980, highlighted the harvest supper, a function marred by the appearance of some young trouble-makers. However, aggravation on the rustic scene produced an unlikely heroine ...

Mornin' ter orl on yer. We wuzzer cummin' up ter Norridge larst Satterday ter tearke a garp at thole City ginst Barmingham, but Ted Daynes sed he coont ford it, cors heez on the dool, so we hed a little seshun down the Datty Duck an' then went hoom an' slept it orff afore the harvist supper.

Thass a real good dew in the Rectory Rum, an' they dunt mynd a bitter beer arter the preers an' searler goods. Wimmun git the dwiles owt an' cleer up when parsin git up on the cheer, put his ole hans tergether an' bless us orl fer stickin' at it in the filds, an' that ent long afore them mawthers are hossin' rown the floor and the kids a' gallawantin' frutter thole rekud player.

That wuz goin' on real nyce Satterday at bowt harparst ten. Wuh, even that Mrs. Elliott-Smythe wuz hevin' a go at the palley glide, and sheez ewsewally tew stuck up ter git orff har seat an' joyn in the merrymint wi' rest onnus. They rekun sheer bin lot better since har ole man past on. She keep 'em in orda at parish cownsil an' help wi' flour rearnjin at the chach. She weer them funny gret ole hats wi' frewt stuck on top onnem. Oim bit sprized wun or tew hent bin orkshuned orff. Cloddy Gates say theers nuff grub fer a munth on topper har skull if yew feel like nickin on' it. He wuz a gorta give har a tinner that Coronearshun milk wun nite when he wuz fulla davilment. Sheeda gi' him sum frewt if he hed dun! Ennyhow, they wuz orl a darnsin' ter wunner them ole songs an' Passy Grimshaw wuz orgnizin' raffel fer a nyce takkey when Jiggy

She cort Jiggy marsters dinger the lug, an he went down lyke a sacker rotten spuds. Her ole dander wuz up.

Ames an' that lot from up the rood tanned up fulla booze an' lookin' fer aggrevearshun.

Theyd bin ter Swoffham Stoons, an yew cood tell they hant cum in fer a sandwidge an' a mardle. They stanker beer, an' wun clyent in a lether jackit towld Norman on the door theyd cumter lyven things uppa bit. They watted summer that punk stuff or suffin', an wunt lissun when parsin say that wuz nearla tyme ter pack up an go hoom ter bed.

Passy Grimshaw arsked Jiggy if heed lyker ter dror the winnin' tickut owter cardbord box, but that wuz orl a bit tense when the whool lot went flyin' crors the flor. Summer the kids wuz blarrin', an' that dint dew no good atorl when ole Alec Fulcher cum charjin' owter the kitchin a' rollin his sleev up wi' a dishclorth over his showlder, an that wuz a drippin' all down his weskut.

Cor blarst me, he let itter them, sayin' they hent got no rite ter go muckin' up uther peples' entertearnmint, an' if they dint sling thar hook, heed gi' them wot for! Wuh, Jiggy's lot jest stood theer tearkin' the ryse owter poor ole Alec, whyle he git moor an' moor earirated. They corl him Grandad an' lotter uther things that dunt bare repetishun. He wunt harfer jifflin' an' swettin' when that Mrs. Elliott-Smythe storked itter middel o' the floor wi' wunner them bloomin' gret marrers wot sheed bort in the searle. She cort Jiggy marsters dinger the lug, an' he went down lyke a sacker rotten spuds. Her ole dander wuz up, an' he muster felt a proppa tewl. Bitser marrer went orl over the plearse, an' she set bowt rest onnem. Thet looked bit lyke Norridge Markit at ender the day, an' even ole parsin wuz tryin' whooly hard not ter bast owt larfin'. Jiggy an' his meartes slunk orf, and they sewn had mewsic on the go gin. They sung "Sheez Jolla Good Feller!" for Mrs. Elliott-Smythe, an' towld har she orta go few rowns alonger that Larry Hooms. That orl go ter show, we dunt hatta corl in the coppas when things git a bit humpty in owr willuj. A few moor gals lyke har, posh hats anorl, theyd sewn sort owt them yung hellyuns in that Barklay Stand!

Oill hev nuther little yarn wiyyer next week. Hang on ter yer marrers cors they mite cum in handy. Mynd how yer go, dunt stick yer snowt in wheer that ent watted, an' dunt yew fergit ... Dew yew keep a' troshin!

EXIT

◇ *ALL DRESSED UP . . .* ◇

Old Barney turned theatre critic when "Oh Calcutta" came to Norwich in October, 1980. Radio Norfolk's talented rural correspondent gave his views in the Dinner Time Show on Tuesday, October 7th – hence the change in his traditional greeting –.and the broadcast was repeated on the following Saturday. Clearly, the show made a big impression on him.

Arternewn ter orl on yer. Oi know we live in a parmissive sosiety. Cors theyre got wunner them newd calinders 'hind the bar at the Datty Duck, an' a few onnem are really lookin' forrard ter December when that mawther wi' noffin on sept a smyle an' a bitter tinsel will be gorpin' down at 'em. That sorta stuff's orrite in moderearshun, but that dunt dew ter git tew sited when yer gitter my age. Betta Grearble an' May West gimme pletty o' idears few yeer ago, but yew dunt git much charnse ter put 'em itter practise when yewr choppin' owt or mukspreddin!

Ennyhow, Oi gi' thole pub a miss larst nite an' hossed orf ter the Theetre Royle in Norridge ter hev a garp at that "Oh Calcutter" longer m'ole mearte Cloddy Gates. He wunt tew keen on the idear, cors he rekun he mite bump inter sumwun wot know 'im. Oi towld 'im not ter be ser sorft. If they knew him, heed know them . . . so theer wunt ner poynt in enny on em puttin' on datty Max an' tendin' they wunt theer.

That dew hityer sorta funny when orl them mawthers an' blooks cum on a' singin' an' darnsin' an' lollopin' crorss wun nuther wi' orl that stimilearted sex. But arter bowt har-fanhowr onnit, yew dunt feel qwyte ser sorft. Theyre 'njoyin' onnit up theer, so yew mite's well get on wiyyer Molteezers an' hev a good chow cors yer arnt lowd ter smook.

Thyere binner hevvin' this sorta show up Lunnun fer hel-luva long tyme, an' Cloddy rekun he an' his meartes owter the willuj wunce wet up ter the big city on a bus trip ter the

Winmill. They lorst Billa Sparjin an' Naffy Horkins, an' they dint harf git towld orf when they wuz learter fer milkin' next day! I heer ole Winmill't shut now; thass Datty Duck wot never clouse theez days.

They dew say theer ent ner shearme in showin' orf the hewman body longus yewre hedda good wash fast, an' this heer revew wot Dick Condor he' got runnin' orl week dunt mearke ner boons bowt it. Plettyo 'larfs anorl, thow summer the jooks wuz owld nuff fer Cloddy ter member a' hearin' when he wuz in tharmy. He upset wun ole gal sittin' frutter us by tellin' har how that wuz gowin' ter end for that wuz finished. Mynd yew, Oi hed a good idear wot wuzzer cummin' when that chap went inter chemists wi' a rum complearnt. That emt my job ter be orl deep an phillysoffical. Theers nuffer them educearted fellers tryin' ter mearke a livin' owter that, an' weer got wun or tew knoworl marchants down the pub wot git on that high hoss bowt Commun Markit an' Panrarmer.

But if I wuz arsked ter stick m' finger on orl this heer newd singin' an' darnsin', I spooz Oid hatta say they wuzzer tellin onnus that sex orta be fun. Cloddy say heer hadda few larfs in his tyme, an' thass way that orta be. Mynd yew, that Gladdis Morton wyped smyle orf his dyall wun nite down Datty Duck when he tryed ter work har hoom. She say she dint want nunner that ole skwit, an' hulled ten bob noot at 'im ter pay forl them brown earles heed bunged fer. That larnt him a lessun, an' he bort a new byke wi' orl the munny he searved arter that.

Cummin'-lyke I dew from a chapel fammly, I wunt sartan that'ud be eezy ter sit an' watch suffin' lyke "Oh Calcutter" an orl them clyents wi' noffin on. Dunt git me rong. I ent no prewd. An' I did know that wunt noffin' ter dew wi' Indyan Tearkway.

But yer nivver know how yewre gorta react at siter orl that kwivrin' flesh. Sum mawthers look bloomin' site better when theyre dolled up stedda in thar baffday sewts, an' Cloddy dunt really look finished orf till heer got his buskins on. Still, thass noyce ter see how sum onnem mearke a' livin', an' if people watter see 'em prarnsin' bowt lyke that, let 'em git on wi'it, Oi say.

Oire gotta git down thole lotment this arternewn, an' thass tew cowld ter tackel that job wiowt a gansy on. Dunt matter if yewre got yer clooths on or orf, keep yer pecker up. Theyre gotta good foller up at the Theetre Royle next week arter all this newdity. Theyre a' dewin a play corled "Datty Linnen" by Tom Stopowt. Praps theyll send free tickets ter Windhum Lorndry. See yer gin' for long. Mynd how yer go. Keep warm if that git bit dark over Wills Muthers, an' arsk Cloddy if he watta be wunner them unnercover ajents! Wotever weather we hev, wun thing yew musn't fergit ... Dew yew keep a' troshin!

*Blarst me, if theer wunt sum funna ole fearses when they sore wot
Cloddy'd nicked owter Stanley's shud . . .*

The changing face of Norfolk village life is one of Old Barney's favourite themes, and he has some sharp things to say about newcomers who make little or no attempt to mix with the locals. Of course, it takes time to become accepted in a rural community, but certain events can break the ice and bring people together. Like having a new village sign.

Mornin' ter orl on yer. That ent tew eezy a' keepin' tracker orl woss gowin' on in the willuj these days. Theers lotta new fearces in thole plearse sinse they bilt them bunglows nexter cownsil howses near the shop. Sum onnem dunt zakkly mix wi' us wotta lived heer orl owr lyves. I dunt think thass allus cors thyere stuck up an' lardydar. Thass morter dew wi' way thyere bizzy gittin' on wi' thar wak in Norridge in them orffices. They cleer orf in the mornins, an' dunt cum owt ner moor when they git hoom. Spooz they garp at the teller-wishun moost nites, an then hoss orf in thar moters weekends.

Rum lyfe if yer arsk me, an' we hent gotta lot in commun. Wunner them blooks woss a slizter or suffin' portant did cum itter Datty Duck thuther nite, but he sewn dunner bunk when Cloddy Gates started a' imiteartin' way he clacked. Wuzzer bit posh, an' we hatta larf when Cloddy twisted his dyall bowt an' took the jewse when he arsked fer nuther pynter myld an' packeter solted nuts.

Ennyhow, real poynter orl this heer is summer them inter-loppers iiter willuj rekun we orta hev wunner them fansa synes put up on the green frutter thole duck pond. That orl started wi' that Jewblee Cummittee wot organised that theer bunfite we hed in Rectory Rum when few onnem got bit moore booze intew 'em than wuz good forrem. Cloddy wunt slow gittin' up ter' bar fer a pynt or tew, an' he say that wuzzer good idear, cors he wuz harf cut an' hent got ner moor munny fer next rownd. Cloddy rekun he knew a carver in the next

willuj wot dew the job fer noffin', and sum mawther say that
wuz jest the job cors that would volve a local crarftsman.

We dint wak that owt at the tyme, but Cloddy wuzzer
yappin' on bowt Stanley Corston, who muster retyred bowt
seventy yeer 'go. He ent proppa senyle, but I wunt trust 'im
wi' wunner them chizzels on a dark nite. Heer had three
wyves wot we know bowt, an' oonly tew onnem are still
moochin' bowt.

They hedda meetin', an' on carstin' wootes cheerman that
wuz greed ter commishin ole Stanley ter git on wi' it. Cloddy
hatta go an' tell him cors he dint know noffin 'bowt it, an' I
wuz roight sprized when Stanley say heed hevva go longas
there wuz few jars innit. Nowun aktewlly towld him wot sorta
syne they watted, thow parsin say thatud be nyce if that hed a
raral flearvour wi' a boinder or a hoss or tew onnit. Darft
thing wuz that cum ter day when the syn orta be unvayled
afore cummittee thowt 'bowt gorta see Stanley. He wunt at
hoom, wuz he. Naybors rekun heed gonter see his sister at
Downham Markit, an cattans wuz drord. A dorg hed messed
up his frut doorstep. That hant bin distarbed, so we knew he
wunt 'bowt. Cloddy say they mite's well hev a snowt rown his
ole shud ter see if the syn wuz theer, an' arter theyd kicked
door open he hollered ter say that wuz in the corner. He
hulled a sack over 't, an' cum hossin' owt fuller bizness an say
they orta git back sharpish if they watted ter be theer fer the
fishul serremuny. They orl belted back ter the lorry wot wuz
weartin' near the gearte, chucked it on an driv orf ter the
green wheer lotter peeple wuz congregeartin' frutta the pond.
Sum hy-up from Districk Cownsil wuz theer ter pull the roop
an' he stand theer orl togged up wi' his chearner orfise an'
smart new hat. They orl started clappin' when Cloddy an'
Biffo Barnard hawled syn orf backer the lorry. I coont see
how that wuz spoozed ter stand up onnits own, but nowun
wuz tickerly bothered. They wuz jest greartful that'd tanned
up atorl.

Sack wuz still onnit when this cownsil blook started yappin'
bowt mewnty spirit, an give a wooter thanks ter deer ole
Stanley Corston wot'd dun itorl as a learbour o'luv. Then that
wuz tyme ter yank the roop. But that got stuck, an' Cloddy
hatta git his shutnife owt ter help. "We hev lift-orf!" hallered

wunner the kids. Orf cum the sack. Blarst me, if theer wunt sum funna ole fearses when they sore wot Cloddy'd nicked owter Stanley's shud ...

That wuz a newd mawther on topper a' bad barfwi' a bowenarrer or suffin' lyke it in har hands. Stanley wuz repearin' onnit fer the feller wotter gotta lotter lorries in his willuj. Blook from the cownsil wunt oonly wun ter feel a proppa tewl!

Cloddy say heed buyer syn owter his own pokit wheer he keep his shutnife he wuz so barrassed. Enny how, they did git rite wun orffa Stanley the nexter week. That wuz in his kitchin dryin' orf whyle he wuz away.

Theeryar then ... weer gotta new syn' an' Cloddy ent brook. Oill hev nuther littel yarn wiyyer next week. Mynd how yer go. Keep thole sack on topper wot yet dunt want them uthers ter see. And dunt yew fergit ... Dew yew keep a' troshin!

*There wuz helluva whoosh as suffin' flew parst his lugs an' jest mist
Cloddy who wuz howldin back cors I rekun he wuz moor sceared
than enny onnus.*

◇ *ROCKET FOR GIBBY* ◇

Youngsters getting up to mischief – such a rich source of rural yarns. Old Barney's village is no exception, and he seems to take a certain delight in relating this story of a prank that caught out Gibby Painter and other Datty Duck regulars. Broadcast on October 18th, 1980.

Mornin' ter orl on yer. Heyya notised how th'nytes are pullin' in? Cor, that oont be long afore weer stookin' up thole fyre arter choppin' wood owter the back, an' dewin' nyce bitter toost ter hev wissum drippin' whoile thass snowin' an' blowin' owtsyde. Yew carnt beet't, speshlly arter yewre hadda good ole blowowt dinner tyme wi' stew an' dumplins. I lyke my grub, an' thass whooly 'portant ter git pletty down on' yer when that start tannin' cowld.

Orl them fewls wot git the flew an' runny snowts sewn's the wind chearnje dreckshun, thass cors they hent got ner go innem. They dunt eat regglar. They pick an' prod an' pingle stedda gittin stuck itter sum good olefashund grub. They dunt harf pull a dyall when yew say yew lyke tearters mashed up wi' a nyce sweed, or a panner fryed unyuns longer yer bearcun on a Sunda mornin'. Wuh, I hent bin leard up fer twetty yeer or moor, an' mooster my ole meartes arnt the sort ter dip owter suffin jest cors thyre gotta skullearke or a bitter gut trubble. If yew keep gowin, yew dunt hatter start gin when yer dunt feel lyke it . . . so thass allus best ter keep gowin, ent it?

I wuz hevvin a yap wi' Cloddy Gates thuther nite arter gearmer crib wi' Gibby Painter. He wun's ewsyual an mearde harfer myld larst bowt cuppel o' howrs for he slid orf hoom crors Norton Fild an' down back learn. He went arly cors he hent bin tew sharp leartely, and we rekun thass orl down ter his ole womun who ent a lotter cop in the kitchen. She even bann hot worter, an' larst tyme she med sum plum jam fer willuj feart, theer wuz fyve unconfarmed cearses o' fewd poysnin the week arter.

Gibby hent gotter lotta meet onnim, an' they say a good breeze'd breark 'm in harf. Ennyhow, me an' Cloddy wuz jest gowin downter Jimmy Gladwin's fer sum chips when Gibby cummer spufflin' back ter the pub lookin' lyke deaf wormed up. Belt wuzzer hangin' orf his coot, an' his ole cap wuz on the huh. We axed him wot wuz up, an he say nowun'd paggarter wot he wuzzer tellin' on' em cors he wuz thoonly wun woted sin it.

Cloddy say they wuz bownd ter be septikle till he towld 'em wot it wuz orl bowt. Gibby tooker swigger the brandy sumbody had bunged fer, an say he wuz sartan that wunt no airyplaine nor a bonfyre over the hidlands.

"I tellya bor, that muster bin wunner them meeteyoroites cummin down owter the sky, an' that wunt far shorta Pendell's haystacks nyther. Theer wuz sum rum noyses anorl, and that feer med me hoss back heer. Weed better ring perlise or sumwun and git 'em ter' vestigayte."

Gibby wuz still a' shearkin', an that dint help when that tewl of a show orf, Jeremy Spindlehurst, hatta put his spook in an' say suffin bowt wizters from nuther planet. Cloddy sewn towld'm ter git on wi' his speers vearders up corner, an' leeve real wald ter them wot could handel onnit. Sum onnem dint watter ring perlise cors they knew that'd put kybosh on bitter learte drinkin'. So we trundled orf longer Gibby ter plearse where he say suffin' big 'n' brite hed cum hossin' down an' put the wind up on 'im.

"Are yew sure that wunt John Bond sendin' signal ter Sir Arfur arskin' him ter sort owt that compensearshun lark longer Canearys?" say Cloddy, tryin' ter cheer orl onnus up. Gibby towld him not ter be ser sorft ... and then theer wuz helluva whoosh as suffin' flew parst his lugs an' jest mist Cloddy who wuz howldin' back cors I rekun he wuz moor sceared than enny onnus. Booth onnem went down, wi' Cloddy hollerin' bowt them Rushins gittin' heer afor heed bilt a shelta. Nifty Wright, wot'd bin in the Hoom Gard, say they orl orta goter grownd an weart fer reyinfossments. Gibby look'd sif he coud dew wi' sum brown trowsers, and then that orl went qwyet til we hard sum larfin ahynd the hidje bowt

26

thatty yard away, an' a loder kids cum bastin' owt, showtin' an' stickin' thar fingers up's they belted trew the gearte an' down the rood.

Yeh, they wuz startin' arly fer Bonfyre Nite, an' poor ow Gibby hatta bleeve't when Nifty fanged howlder dud rockit an say that wuz a rear pitta they hent got noffin betta ter spen' thar munny on. We orl felt bit darft, and dint bother ter ringup Reardyo Norfik an' tellum weed sin suffin' streanje in the sky. But Gibby wunt cum back ter Datty Duck for a qwuickun for he toddled orf ter meet missus owter bingo. Dunt spooz he towld har much bowt't atorl.

Mynd how yer go. Keep yar oiys opin fer the rockits, an' stick yer fingas in yer lugs if theers Littel Deymun bowt. Oill hev nuther littel yarn wiyyer next week. Keep yer powder dry – and dew yew keep a' troshin!

"Howld owt yar hand," she say – and blarst that ewsed ter mearke yer fingers an' nuckels sing when that rewler cum down.

While Old Barney can chuckle over youngsters' pranks, providing they don't carry a malicious edge, he feels they have an easy time at school these days compared with life in the classroom when he was a lad. And Cloddy Gates can relate at least one instance when bad behaviour brought sharp justice. Broadcast on October 25th, 1980.

Mornin' ter orl on yer. Old Barney heer fer bitter a' clack if yew kin speer the tyme. Thass bin rear ole shugarbeetin' weather, hent't, wi' wind, rearn an' mud a' channin' ole filds itter a' kwogmyre. Oim whooly glad I dunt hatter git owt theer wi' sack rown m' middel danglin over m' boots, an' the worter drippin' down bottumer m' ole overawls.

That ent lotter fun, I kin tellyer, an' thass a wunder them ole rewmatix hent sin orl onnem orf. Arter harf howr on the lotment these days, Ire had nuff – even if sun's owt fitt ter bast. I dunt spooz them kids wot go tcr the willuj skool'll finish up on the land. Sum on' em cood dew wi' tearster stoon pickin', haycartin' or bad-scarin' ter larn em how bloomin' eezy they hev things terday. They dunt know theyre born, moost onnem. They git dropped orf in the pleargrownd, rapped up in cotton wool, an' then stand theer a' gorpin' trew th' rearlins weartin' fer sumwun ter collect 'em. Thass searme wi' hollerdays . . . they dunt git stuck inter arn few bob twords new skool clobber. Theyr a ryte sissy lot if yer arsk me, and that dunt payter ding 'em rown the lughool no moor neether. Yew git rong, dunt yer? An' thass why theyre littel hellyuns, allus a' cheekin' an' tiddlin' rownd at hoom an' in the clarsrum.

Weer got wunner them lardydar skoolmarsters in the willuj, streart from ewnivarsity. Heer gotter good d'gree or suffin', that Mister Norton hev, but that dunt stop them kids givin' him sum hard. He say theyere uninhabited an' jest givin' way ter that natrewl feelins. Well, that dunt seem tew natrewl ter me to let onnem muck bowt lyke they dew. Cor blarst, ole Miss Corbett'd tann in har grearve if she cood see the littel blyters a' tearkin' the micky an' hullin' things crors the room stedda keepin' thar snowts in a book an' payin' tenshun ter the rytin' on the blackbord.

She wuz a rum ole gal wi' har black shorl an' lil' ole glarses, parched up on har desk nexter the pypes. If yew spook owter tann, sheed holler for yer ter cum owter the frunt. That wuz yar lott. "Howld owt yar hand!" she say – and blarst that ewsed ter mearke yer fingas an' nuckels sing when that rewler cum down.

Cloddy wuz a tellin' on me how he refewsed ter stick owt his hand wunce when she cort him a pinshin' Mearsy Wilkins' ink. Ole gal dint go leery or noffin. Cloddy hatter stay in arter rest onnem had gone hoom, an' that wuz royte in middel o' the winter tarm. Cloddy wuz spoozed ter git streart hoom an' chearnje so he cood help his farther longer the milkin' cors the farmer hisself was leard up.

That gotta harparst four, an' ole Miss Corbett wuz still moochin' bowt ignorin' Cloddy a' shearkin' an' blarrin' at backer the clarss. Then she started a' markin' the books, an pylin' 'em up in frut onner so she gradewlly dispeered ahind onnem. Cloddy watted a wee, but he dassent arsk if he cood go. He sit theer a' jifflin' an' snifflin' till gone fyve. Then Miss Corbett storked crorss t'him and say she hev better things ter dew than stan' gard over unrewly li'l boys when that wuz tyme fer har tee an' skoons.

"Yew kin go, Gates, an' I hope yew are sewtibly chastised by yar peerants fer bein' ser learte." Cor, he belted down the rood lyke a bat owter hell. But that wuz tew learte ter hurry, an' he gotter ryte solin', fast orf his muther an' then orf his farther fer not helpin' longer the milkin'.

Cloddy rekun he sewn stuck owt his mits when heed binner newsunse arter that! Ole Miss Corbett dint stand fer no messin' bowt, an' orl the kids gotter know it anorl.

Sumwun orter tell that Mister Norton howter sort 'em owt stedda bein' ser sorft. Good dollup o' ole-fashund medsun wunt dew ner harm. We hatter swoller 't, an weer still heer, arnt we? Oill hev nuther li'l yarn wiyyer next week. Mynd

30

how yer go. Dunt pinsh ner' ink if ole Miss Corbett's snowtin' rown', howld owtyer hands an' tearke yer punshmint, an' if that hatter lot, jest yew 'member wot ter dew. Thassit ... yewre got it ... Dew yew keep a' troshin!

◇ *THE DEFECTIVE VAN!* ◇

Playing practical jokes on each other is all grist to the Datty Duck mill, but it's not so funny when the laughs are on you. Old Barney's salutary tale on November 1st, 1980, must have brought purrs of satisfaction from the BBC hierarchy worried at the number of people without a television licence. Cloddy's on the receiving end.

Mornin' ter orl on yer. Are yer lookin' forrard ter Chrismuss? Dunt mearker lotter diffrunse if yer arnt, dew it? Orl that skwit in the winders longer that imitershun snow – and we hent hed firewak nite yit! Wuh, that dunt seem fyve minnit sinse we wuz hollerin' bowt plowin' the filds an' scattrin'. Now thass bloomin tyme ter stick up the holly an' th' iyvy. Thass wunder the Eester eggs ent on searle anorl ter searve us a' gowin back ter the shops.

I dunno if thass got ennything ter dew wi' this Commin Markit lark, but we dew fear ter be hossin' long wi' owt rearrly knowin' where weer a' gowin'. That crearze me way they stick orl them advertizements on the telly sewn's yewre got yer Chrismuss dinna down on yer. I nivver go on hollerday mesself, an I sartantly wunt wotter go ter wunner them posh hotels wi' orl them mawthers gowin' rown starkers on the beech, an them blooks garpin' at 'em sif that wuz fast tyme theyd sin ennything lyke it. Rum job if yewre gotter go orl that bloomin' way just ter see bitter crumpit ent it?

But Oim gittin' orf the subject. We orl lyke Chrismuss, but we dunt want it bunged down owr troats from harvist tyme onnerds. Cloddy wuzzer tellin' on me bowt sum kids in the willuj wot tapped him up fer a penny fer the guy thuther nite owtsyde Datty Duck. Wun onnem wuz propped up ginst the worl wi' a rockit a' stickin' owter his shat. Cloddy thowt he looked real lyfelyke, an wuz bowt ter chuck cuppel o' bob itter thowld hat when that littel darvil sneezed an ran orf.

Bowt howr learter, Cloddy wuz hevin' bitter grub an' reedin' the pearper when he hard sum singin' owtsyde. Them searme kids wuz givin onnim "Way in a Mearnjer". When he wenter the daw they dint stop ter wish him Yewltyde greetins!

Yew carnt rearly blearme the kids thow, kin yer? Theyre allus on the mearke, and that cum eezy an' go eezy these daze. But they git it from the grownups. Cloddy's a bite tite, an' I dunt jest meen when he stagger owter the pub rown' closin' tyme. He got the wind up when we hard that defective van wuz cumin' rown ter see if yewre gotter tellerwishun lysense. Dunno how they kin see threw the cattans if yewre wotchin' culler or blackanwite, but there hev bin bitterer parje on in the distrik.

Cloddy ent oonly wun livin' on rong syder the lore, but he is a bitterer ole wurryguts. Sorft tewl towld 'em orl down the pub dittee that heed hatter brake itter his sayvins ter git a lysense. Well, heed a' dun betta ter keep his trap shut ...

Daffy Hoskins, whoos bitofa larf when heez sober, thowt thated be good idear ter pay Cloddy a visit wun nyte larst week when he wuz a' wotchin "This is Yar Lyfe". Cloddy hev snowt cearse Aymon Andrews fang howlder him an tell us orl wot a wunnerful sort o' chap he is. Ennyhow, Daffy pulled owld trilby over his skull an' wynded gret ole black scarff rown his cearke hole. He hed sum dark glarsses anorl, an' he looked lyke wunner them spize owter the pitchers as he storked up ter Cloddy's frunt daw an' givver littel tap. Cloddy jest bowt messed hisself when Daffy say he wuz from the tellerwishun peeple sortin' them owt wot hent gotter lysense.

Cloddy rekun that wuz jest oversite, an' he wuz fixin' up ter git ter the poost orffice fast thing next mornin'. Daffy say heed giv' im twetty foor howr ter cumply wi' regulearshuns – and cleered orf down the pub. Well, we wuz larfin' fitter bust when Cloddy cum in an arsk fer lemunearde shandy. "Woss that orl yew kin afford?" say Daffy, an' bort him a proppa pynt. That wuz wath it, wunt it?

Oill hev nuther littel yarn wiyyer next week. Mearke sattan yewre orrite cearse that defective van cum rown yors! Mynd how yer go. Git yer horryzontul howld rite, and dunt yew fergit. ... Dew yew keep a' troshin!

The dangers of nuclear war are just as important a topic for discussion in Old Barney's village as the price of beer, changes in the weather or new toilets in the pub. And his rural report of November 8th, 1980, underlined the way his local community had to get to grips with one of the global problems of the day.

Mornin' ter orl on yer. Ent tew sartan I orter say a lot bowt woss bin gowin' on in the willuj cearse that go ginst that Fishul Sekruts Act or suffin. Yew dunt know whooz keepin' thar lugs ter thole grown these daze, dew yer? Theers orl them C an' A earjunts moochin' bowt, an them Russhins weartin' ter show that filem star blook in Americca wheer ter git orf. Mynd yew, that Ronuld Raygun look jest the sorter chap ter tell them wheer ter stick thar missyles. He put the wind up me a bit, I kin tellyer!

Parsunally, I carnt see ner poynt in blowin' orl onnus ter bits, an I rekun that Marster Cosyjin an' his lot in the Crumlin wood be proppa sorft ter go pushin' buttins when theyre gotter cleer the mess up tharselves.

Ennyhow, they hadder meetin' in the rektry rum this week ter git us reddy fer wunner them newcleeer disarsters. That Missus Smythe-Elliott wuz in the cheer, orl dun up lyke a dawg's dinner in wunner har gret big hats an' a far coot wot she bort when har ole man pegged owt. Wuh, she went on bowt the Red Perul an' that Iyron Mearden woss gorter put orl on em in thar plearse. She wuz chuntrin' on bowt NATO when Gibby Pearnter axed har if that stood fer Norridge Arnt Tew Organysed. She dint git the drifter that, cors she ent tew rapped up longer footbawl, an' Bilko Butterfield say he wotted ter mearke pynt o' order. Cloddy say he wotted pynt o' myld, but orl on em hatter howld thar slarver when Nifty Wright – woss bin in the Hoom Gard – git up an mearke propersihun we orter bild a fawl owt shelta owter munny wot theyer med owter bingo. Parsun dint seem tew keen on whool bizness, cors he thowt that munny wuz fer sum new cattans in the westry an thole peeples owtin ter Yarmuff in the summer. But he dint put his spook in whyle Nifty wuz sayin' how much grub we orter tearke itter the shelta, and how portant that wuz ter hev pletty ammernishun cearse them Jarmans tryed ter brearke in. He wuz gittin' ryte wakked up, an' nowun hed the hart ter tell on 'im larst wor wuz over an dun with.

We hatter voot afore that wuz tyme ter git the tearbles owt fer bingo an' lock up, an moost onnus thowt that wuz best ter leeve the raynjments ter Missus Smythe-Elliott an har lot on the Parish Cownsil. Thyere gorter rite ter the Govinment ter see if we kwolify fer a grarnt, seeins how weer a raral mewnity wi' owt lotter pook cummin' in.

Cloddy rekun we orter bild the shelta ahind the Datty Duck cors lot onnus are moost lykely ter be hevin' a jar when them Crewd Missyles cum hossin' over. Bet he dunt volunteer ter nip owt an' git next rownd in! Lanlord say we orter keep whool thing sekrut cors theer myte be wunner them mowls in the willuj a' wakkin' fer the Commernists. He shunt paggarta orl that skwit in the parpers. Oonly mowl weer got thass underneef my lotment!

Well, Oill hev nuther littel natter wiyyer next week, if we hent orl bin blowed ter kingdom cum. Mynd how yer go, and dunt yew fergit down theer in the shelta ... Dew yew keep a' troshin!

◇ *PANTOMIME FUN* ◇

Norwich Theatre Royal sets a rousing example when it comes to pantomime spectaculars – and artistic inspiration has seeped through to many Norfolk village groups. These lines, broadcast on Saturday, November 15th, 1980, give the cue for dramatic developments in Old Barney's parish – although he's no performer!

Mornin' ter orl on yer. Ire hadder gutfull o' this heer wether, hent yew? Black iyce, sleet an' rearn wi' that learzy ole win' blowin' streart trew yer. That tearke a blook orl his tyme ter git hoom from the pub in wun bit. I nearla cumma cropper orffer moy byke thuther nite, an' that wunt jest cors weed bin hevvin tew menny sharbits down the Datty Duck. That wuz Cloddy's bathday or suffin', so that wuz pritty qwyet orl rown. He say ole yeers are rowlin' rown tew sharpish fer him ter dew alotter selebreartin'.

I know wot he meen. Yew git ter the poynt when yew wotter nite frutter the fyre stedda gollopin orf ter darts matches or gearmer crib. An yew git up tyred in the middel o' winter, dunt yer, when yewre hadder bitterer larf nite afore. I git them rewmatix now an' gin anorl, an that ent no fun when yewre gotter lotter bykin' ter dew.

Few on 'em in the willuj he' got the flew, so that put bitterer kybosh on rehearsals fer that Chrismuss pantomyme in larst cuppel o' weeks. They're a' dewin "Robertson Crewsoe", an kids down the skool hev bin bizzy mearkin' lotter parm trees an' things lyke that forra sorta tropikal settin'. They dunt dew bad tann neether, that lot in the dramatik syety, thow summer them mawthers wot rekun they kin sing'd be better orf in a cats kwire! They yorp suffin' wicket, an boys wuz stickin' cottin wool in thar lugs larst year when they wuz dewin' "Sindarella". Suffin' went rong wi' the gyant pumpkin anorl, and cattans dint pull proppa when that yung warmint Sniffy Hall let roops slip trew his hans.

*Kids down the skool hev bin bizzy mearkin' lotter parm trees an'
things lyke that forra sorta tropikal settin'.*

He hent got the job this tyme, and theyere formed proppa cumittee ter deel wi' searler tickuts. Thass cors theer wuz helluva slarver larst yeer when sum o' them lokal hyups coont git in on the nyte at the daw. Plearse wuz full, an Mearjor Comptun-Bracket an' his ole gal dint fanser a' sprorlin' tharselves owt on the flaw at the back. Thar lot hatter cleer orf, an' they dint send ner raffel pryzes fer the big tombola arter Chrismuss.

This heer "Robertson Crewsoe" hev bin ritten by that Mister Norton wot larn kids at the willuj skool, an' cuppel o' his meartes frum ewnivarsity wot he keep in tuch with. Cloddy he' sin the skript lyke, an' he rekun theers sum good larfs innit. He wuz a' tellin' on Mister Norton a jook thuther nite he say he orta ewse in that pantomyme. Wuh, that wen' down lyke tunner bricks. Cloddy say: "Why did Robertson Crewsoe hev evvra weekind orf?" Mister Norton, he din' know tharnser ter that wun. "Thass cors he had orl his wakk dun ber Fryday!" say Cloddy, bustin' owt larfin' an' pokin' 'im in the ribs. I dunno if Mister Norton is thick or wot, but he say that wuz tew suttel fer the lokal ordyances. Cloddy still rekun thass a good-un . . . but weer orl hard it now hent we?

Stanley Philby dunt help much when he keep chuntrin' on bowt dressin' up lyke Bownty Barr ter give the perduckshun a bitter flearvur. Sum onnem dunt zakkly show rite sorter attitewd, but thass sartan ter be sellowt agin.

They hev arsked me if I wotted wunner them bit parts. Wuh, I dunno how yew player bit, an' I ent ner cop at 'memberin' lynes. When I wuz a kid at Sunny Skool, we hatter larn resitearshuns fer th' annyvarsry, an' I wuz allus larst wun ter git ole vasses in m' skull. No, I ent no akter, an' Oill leeve orl that ter them wot lyke gittin' up theer'n performin. That orl pend now how kwick that flew bug cleer orf. Yew carnt hev reharsal longer three onyer, kin yer? Thass lyke gowin' ter footbawl match an' oonly wun teem tan up. Mynd yew, that'd help Norridge owter thar littel trubble if they dint hev no oppersishun.

Well, Oill be back ter hev nuther li'l natter wiyyer next week. Mynd how yer go, git yer lynes rite, an member wot that Willyum Spookshearve allus ewsed ter say . . . Dew yew keep a' troshin!

DATTY
DUCK

◇ *CLODDY'S ROMANCE* ◇

Cupid can strike in the most unlikely places, but imagine the wagging tongues and shaking heads down at the Datty Duck when Cloddy Gates, seemingly a confirmed bachelor, turns up with a lady on his arm. News of this romantic liaison was given to an unsuspecting Norfolk on November 22nd, 1980.

Mornin' ter orl on yer. Thass Ole Barney heer wi' bitter lokul skandel. Cloddy hebbin' an' got hisself bitter stuff! Dunno if that Miss Wald bizness sorter tanned his brearn an' put ideers itter his skull or wot, but heer brook habits of a lyfetyme an' started bringin' this mawther, down Datty Duck. An' he borter Babysham wi' cherry pokin' owt onnit, so that must be sorter seryus.

We orl thowt he wuz a man's man, an boyz down crickut club hent harf got the wind up cearse they hatter fynd sum-wun else t' umpyre next seezun. Cloddy's a lyfe member, so he dunt hatter pay no prescripshun, an' they thowt heed be owt theer till he droppt or run owter stoons.

He hent sed noffin' fishul, but I carnt see this heer bloom lettin' him tiddel bowt orl weekind. She ent noffin' speshal, I spooz, but sheer gotter few bob an' har own plearse on that new stearte neer the chach. She ewsed ter be seketary ter wun o them bizness blooks up Norridge afore she packt it in ter look arter har farther. He dyed few munth ago, an' I rekun she started a' feelin' har feet agin. We thowt suffin' mite be in th' wind when Cloddy say he coont git ter the darts meetin' thuther week, but that wuz stiller sprize when he cum prarnsin' itter the pub larst Tewsday wi' this heer mawther orl dolled up an hangin' otter tharm o' his ole coot.

"Heyyer bort yer arrers wiyyer?" say Gibby, nudjin rest onnus up at the bar. "No, that I hent," say Cloddy, puttin' har far stool longer the rester har clobber onter the peg nexter the toylet daw. That stanker moffbawls, an' har neckluss looked

41

She ent noffin speshal, I spooz, but sheer gotter few bob an' har own plearse on that new stearte neer the chach.

sif thatted jest dropt owter wun o' them Chrismuss crackers wot yer pay hellanorl for.

"No," say Cloddy agin, "me an' Lucy are gowin' owt fer a meel arter weer hadder kwyet drink. Thass har bathday. Sheez Skorpyun, yer know." Gibby hadder job notter bast owt larfin. He mutter "Yeh, bilt lyke a tank anorl!" Cloddy dint heer 'im, an' they cleered orf when they'd dun. She ett har cherry anorl, an' dawbed summer that lipstik an' powder rown har chops. Gibby say yet carnt improov thole pitcher ber puttin' new frearme rown' onnit, an' I know wot he meen.

We think Cloddy hebbin' batchler orl his lyfe, thow he did hev a gal on the go jest arter the wor. She sorter dispeered inner hurry lyke, an they rekun she wenter Lunnun ter git better job. Sinse then Cloddy hebbin wunner the lads, an nivver thowt heed finish up at his earje workin' sum mawther owt an' givin' har that sorft look wot yer see down the darnse an' the pitchers when them yunguns are fangin' howlder eech uther.

Wuh, he must be well parst it now ... fifty far or suffin' ... but I spooz yew hatter give inter yer moshuns howivver owld yar. I hent stopt lookin', an yet git sum tearsty gals down that playskool. I think theyere sorter flattened when yew garp attem an say "How dew yew dew?" in yer best voyce. But I shunt wotter be trucked up wi' wun onnem. Blarst me, no! They arsk wheer yer bin when yew git hoom learte wi' few jars insyde yer, an' they dunt unnerstand when yewre gotter go ter darts match afore the woshin ups dun. No, theyere orrite in thar rite plearse, an that ent in my howse. I ent tew sartan Cloddy's sorted it orl owt yit. Rekun next thingull be 'gearjment party down Datty Duck. Then heel hatter git rownd in!

Oill be back fer nuther little yarn longonyer next week, if I hent got mesself nyce bitter stuff anorl. Mynd how yer go – speshly if yew are marryed – and dunt fergit ter tell 'em when they arsk yer bizness. Thassit, bor ... Dew yew keep a' troshin!

He flew crors the snow, an' tript up sum blook gorpin attim owtsyde the bredshop daw.

Every village has its legendary snow story, ready for another airing as soon as the big flakes start to fall. The epic trek of 1963 is a firm favourite with the Datty Duck regulars, not least because they just beat their rivals from a neighbouring village to the bakery for much-needed supplies of new bread. Old Barney used his loaf on November 29th, 1980.

Mornin' ter orl on yer. Whooly good ter see the snow this week wunt it? Give thole plearse Chrismuss card look, but that ent ner fun if yewre tryin' ter hoss long on yer byke. I carnt ford rayndeer, an' thass long wile sinse I took sledje owter thole shud.

Spooz thass orrite fer the kids, but they sewn git fed up when thar lugs tann blew an' they start blarrin' o' cowld. They git sooked trew arter snowbawl fyte, an' then chuck thar clobber orl over the howse. Little hellyuns git way wi' marder thees daze, speshlly when they stick stoons an' rox sider the snow afore hullin onnit. Thass dearnjrus, but they dunt think noffin onnit till they hat sumwun.

We wuz bangin' owr rubber boots ginst the daw o' the Datty Duck thuther nite cors lanlord wuz muttrin' bowt pools o' worter orl over plearse. Cloddy got nite orf from his bitter stuff, so he started clackin' on bowt tyme willuj wuz cut orf ber blizzud bowt 1963. Cloddy lyke this heer yarn cors he gotter ward or suffin' fer cummin' ter thayd of the striken publik. That orl started when ole win' blew crorss Gregorys filds wheer there ent ner hidjes ner moor, an that filled Red Barn lane rite up in unner a' minnit. We cud see that wuz gorter git ruff when we cum owter pub afore twalve. Snowin' lyke hell an' driftin'. Leest yew could see wheer yew wuz gowin, thow that wunt tew eezy a' gittin' theer. Sum onnem say they orter put up fer the nyte at the Datty Duck cors thated be helluva job mearkin' it back in the mornin. That wuz a reeznubel poynt, but we went orf larfin' an' singin. Wunt lotter larfs bowt next day when yer garped owter the winder. Cor blarst, yer wundered wheer whool wald 'd gone … an' then I sore Cloddy larchin' over wheer ditch wuz, hollerin an' chuckin' his arms rown lyke he wuz a drowndin'.

He fell itter the daw, snow orl rown his snowt an' his eyes a' worterin', an he tryed ter hawl his trowsers up over his boots. "Cum yew on," he say. "Weer gorter belt crors back medders an' git ter Clarkes bearkers shop for orl the bred go. Git moov on; that lot from Chubley'll be theer for us is we arnt ceerful."

Dint rearly know wot he wuz slarvrin' on bowt, but that did sownd arjunt, so orf we go, collectin' sum uther blooks on th' way wot wuz diggin' tharselves owt. That wuz lyke trudjin' ter North Pool, I sink, but we hant got nunner them husky dawgs ter help us. Pinky Waller collupsed itter heep near Philbys Barn, so we chucked sum stror overim an' towld him ter keep still an dunt moov till we cum back. He dint say no so that wuz on wi' owr hazerdus jarnney itter thunown.

Weed nearla med it ter the bearkery when Cloddy let owt helluva showt. Heed sin that lot from Chubley a' cummin' thuther way. "Charje!" he holler. He flew crors the snow, an' tript up sum blook gorpin' attim owtsyde the bredshop daw. That wuz thowner, wunt it, who dint mynd who git theer fast. We pyled in ahind Cloddy an filld sacks up wi new bred. "Weel bung forrit tomorrer!" say Cloddy, cleerin' orf fit ter buster gut. We got hoom four howr arter, fyndin' Pinky Waller still a' moonin' an' groonin' wheer we left thole fewl. Theer wunt ner bred left fer thuther lot, but we dint go tew short while plearse wuz bunged up wi' snow. Them from Chubley got orl the tinned pees, spuds an' kindlin' owt thuther shop wot we hant got tyme ter go to, so they dint starv neether. Cloddy hadder lot drinks bort 'im. Parish Cownsil giv him sum sustifigat fer gittin' back wi' the bred. That still hang in his kitchun, orl frearmed an' swanky lyke on the worl. But we dunt lettim fergit we went crors them filds anorl. Pinky Waller still say heeder meddit if that hant bin snowin.

Well, Oill hev nuther little yarn wiyyer next week if we hent bin bunged up. Mynd how yer go. Git pletty o' bred in cearse that dew tann funny. An' if yer git mer drift, dunt fergit … Dew yew keep a' troshin!

Sounds reasonable . . . anyone in the village caught smoking in the next two weeks will have to make a contribution towards the old folks' Christmas party. Fund-raising with a purpose. But Cloddy is soon fuming at the idea, as our rural correspondent reports, without a cough, on December 6th, 1980.

Mornin' ter orl on yer. Dunno if yewre corfin' an' spluttrin' whyle yewre lissunin' ter this heer, but thass shure thing them ole fags dunt dewyer lotter good.

I ewsed ter git threw thatty corfin nearls a day till a few yeer back when I got pearns in th' chist, an' hedder blakowt wun mornin' when I wuz hedjtrimmin. Cor, that whooly put the win' upper me, I kin tellyer, an' I hossed rester moi packit o' Gowld Fleark itter the fyre when I cum rown.

I did tryer pype fer a tyme, but lyke ole Lilly Potter – thass owr lokal bingo kween – that kep' gowin owt, an' that took helluva lotter stookin up for that wuz enny good. I dunt bother ner moor, but I dunt git onter them wot dew joy a corf an' a spit.

Cloddy rowl his own, an heer allus got bowt yarder ash danglin' owter his gob or droppin down his perrile pullover. Ire herd him a barkin' an' brawchin' fast thing in th' mornin, and he say he hevver fawler soot wunce a week. Spooz he git trew tew ownses o' Owld Holburn a day, an' he dassent go when that chisty-ray mobyle ewnit cum rown owrs larst yeer. We towld onnim that wunt penentreart trew his army coot an' weskut, but he say theers sum things yer just dunt watter know bowt. Gibby Painter went. He dunt smook much, but he new yew git cuppertee arterwards.

Enny how, Cloddy's rite up the snowt cors Ole Peeples Chrismuss Party Cummitee hev cum up wi' good idear ter rearse munny fer this yeers dew. Ennywun in the willuj woss cort hevvin' a drag next cuppel o weeks, theyere gotter bung harf akwid itter the hat. Cloddy dunt kwite kwolyfy fer the party, but we rekun heel pay fer moost onnit less he cut down pritty sharpish. Sewns he dip iiter his pockit fer his baccer an' pearpers at Datty Duck thuther nite, sumwun hollered: "Thatell cors yer nuther boxer crakers, Cloddy!"

He wunt harf irritbull, an' say that wuz gowin ginst orl hewmun rites. When he slid orff fer a tiddel, threen onnem went anorl ter mearke sartan thass orl he did go fer.

His bitter stuff dunt smook, an' she keeper nudjin onnim when he git that look crors his dyall an' start moochin' rown' orl sorrerful lyke.

Parsun he' formed a willujanty groop ter keeper eye on them wotter on the weed. Thass orl in good cawse, he say, but heez lukky he hent got dinger the lug or tew way heer bin gowin on. He follered ole gals hoom arter whist dryve thuther nite, an stuck his cullexshun box owt when he jump trew the hidje an' put the Whooly Goost up onnem. Dunt think he gotter lot, sept few sujjestyuns wheer he mite like ter stick it.

Cloddy sad heed putter fyver in if they left him loon, an' thass on jender fer nex' mitty meetin'. For then, heer gotter keep bungin if he git cort, an' theer arnt menny plearses wheer he kin twist wun up wiowt been sin. Sum kids wuz snowtin' in his kitchun winder larst nite when he wuz gittin' fit fer strowl down pub. They started yorpin' an' bangin' when he went fer matches in his jackit, an' poorl ole bugga jest bowt hadder hart tack. That ent no fun tryin' ter dew wot cum natrul rown heer, an' I shunt be sprized if Cloddy dunt sling his hook an' go on hollday fer week or tew. Trubbel is he need the munny ter keep him in fags!

Oill hev nuther littel natter wiyyer next week. Dunt smook tew much, cut down ifyer kin, an' dunt cadje 'em if yer wotter give up. Mynd how yer go ... and dunt yew fergit. ... Dew yew keep a' troshin!

◇ *RED FACE FOR CLODDY* ◇

Old Barney has already given us several examples of how Norfolk people have their own way with words. "Sustifigat" is but one amusing corruption of "certificate", and it can vary from one home to another. There are no firm rural rules! On December 13th, 1980, we hear how Cloddy got in a right old muddle over his raffle prize. Some pronounced him a fool ...

Mornin' ter orl on yer. Heyya dun yer Chrismuss shoppin' yit? Crearze yer, dunt it, orl that pushin' an' shuvin' when yew go jest ter fang 'older sum arter-shearve, boxer chocluts an' few things ter trikuleart thole tree. Summer them mawthers hent got minnit ter live, an' theyre spoozed ter be shorter munny! Allus seem ter fynd it when that cum ter bungin' fer Chrismuss.

An' kids git on yer wick, blarrin' fer suffin they carnt hev. I saw wun littel hellyun in Jarrelds thuther day kickin' up proppa fuss cors he wotted wunner them trearn sets wot go full pelt an' tearke up harf the frunt room. His ole womun wunt harf snotty, him a' showin' har up lyke that. She say he mite git it next yeer if he hearve 'isself – sum charnse o' that, I rekun – an' she bort him sum sweets cors he wuz still a' bullerin' when they git orf that moovin' lift. Iyder kicked his littel arse owt onnit an' stuck suffin' reel nyce in his stockin – lyke lumper cool an poysnus sneark. Theez kids think theyere oonly gotter howl an' theyll git wot they wont. Wuh, ent rite issit? Blarst, we dassent git up ter them trix when we wuz smorl or weeder got suffin we hent arsked fer.

We wuz yarnin down the Datty Duck bowt thold daze whyle lanlord kept stickin dror tickuts unner owr snowts. That git on yer chymes anorl. I hent nivver wun noffin, but Cloddy must hevver howsefull o' stuff heer carted orf over the yeers. Heez a jammy begger, an muster bin winnin' things whyle he wuz in the creardel a' slarpin' his Cowan Gearte an' hossin them rusks itter him.

Mynd yew, he dint harf look a tewl few yeer back when he cum beltin' itter the pub an say heed wun a dyvin sewt in a raffell runber the horspittle fun' rearsin' cumittee. Cor blarst, we say, wotyer gorn ter bottom o' the Lillypits longer that Jake Custard? Yew wotter wotch owt fer them resitearshun trubbles when yer git back, an' if yew git the bens, yewd better tearke over in gool fer the willuj footbawl teem. Cloddy dint ceer. He wunt harf a' swankin', an he putton his best sewt when he wenter distribushion o' pryzes jest afore Chrismuss.

His wuz sekund pryze, an he stand theer garpin' mung orl them portent nasses an' dokters wiwoet thar stiffoscoops when his nearme cum up. "Mr. Cloddy Gates. Wood yew pleeze step forrad an' sept wi' owr gratulearshuns yar bewtiful pryze donearted ber Jenkins the Farnitcher Stoors."

What the hell hadder farnitcher stoor gotter dew wi' unnerworter bizness? Cloddy got it rong, dittee ... He hent wun a dyvin sewt ... that wuz smart divann sweet! He dint harf git sum legpullin bowt that. "Woyyer gorter wotch telly wi' snorkul on?" say boys down the pub. "If yewder gotter bed, yew cooder put that at bottum o' the rivver," say sum brite spark. Went on lyke that orl nite, an' Cloddy hent zakkly lived that wun down.

No dowt heel hoss orf wi' moost pryzes down the pub agin when they hev thar dror. Longers he dunt git ner fags an' git cort smookin. Well, Oill hev nuther littel natter wiyyer next week, if yewre gotner breth left arter orl that gallawantin' rown them bloomin shops. Mynd how yer go. Hoop yer tickut cum up for yer dun. If yer dunt hev ner luck, jest yew member wot I allus tellyer ... Dew yew keep a' troshin!

When he arrived at Radio Norfolk on December 20th, 1980, Old Barney was clutching a letter he was bursting to read. A lady listener had fallen under his rustic spell, and she'd sent him some precious memories to share with a growing audience. Countless others have sent letters since – but the first one really tickled Old Barney's fancy.

Mornin' ter orl on yer. Heyyer had nuffer orl this Chrismuss lark for that git heer? Well, Oill giyyer brake an' tellyer bowt my fast fann letter. No, that dint cum from Cloddy neether, an I hent poosted it messell. Coont reed m'own ritin iffer did.

Thass from a nyce mawther wot lyke a bitter Norfik skwit. Sheer binner tellin' me sum yarns bowt thold daze. Wun onnem in tickler cum crors rite well, an' they orl larfed when I towld em down Datty Duck. That go lyke this heer, she say . . .

"Us mawthers lyked harvist tyme, an' ewsed ter carry the dinners an' the farses t'owr farthers an' bruthers in the filds, an wotch 'an' try ter ketch the rabbits when they runned owt when the corn wuz bein cut. We larfed wun day! Jimmy wuz runnin arter wun, an Bob nocked agin him·an he felled down. I axed him, 'Wot are yew blarrin for?' Jimmy say, 'Bob jampt on moy hand an Oid cotched a rabbit. Then she up wi' har lugs an' way she flew.' I say, 'Bor, praps they wuz wings.' He say, 'No, they wuz lugs.' This heer mawther wot rit ter me, she say her muther ewsed ter mearke jinjer pop. Wun day in the harvist fild, farther pulled the cork owter the bottell an' it flewed away. Farther, who wuz the marster wun ter holler, he hollered: 'Git that cork! Git that cork!' Sum sheep hed bin neer the plearse wheer we sit, an' in my flurry I pickt up suffin theyd dropt. Farther comed afore I cood hull it down. He let owt: 'Yew sorft fewl, dunt yew know a cork from a tad! If I hant bin a' lookin' yewder corked by bottell up wi' a tad! Yew hent got happorth o' sense, or a farden wath o' gumpshun!'

Oh farther ... afrunt o' orl thuther mawthers an' boys. They whooly larfed." That tearke yer back, dunt it, littel yarn lyke that? An' if yewre got suffin yewd lyke ter hev on this heer wyrless, jest yew hoss it orf ter Reardyo Norfik. Theyll parsit onter me so I kin hevver garp when I cum orf the lotmint.

I hent dun orl mer shoppin' yit, so Oid betta git on wi'it for the pub opin ternite. Weer gotter littel singsong gowin, an' Cloddy say heel dew a tann if we kin fynd a pianner. A sorter Liberarchy wi' buskins, I rekun. Heer gotter good voyce anorl, an' he lyke them ole songs wot the kids tan thar snowts up at. Yew carnt beet 'em ... wads reely meen suffin. Not lyke orl this punkish skwit. That oont larst willit?

Well, I hoop ter be wiyyer Chrismuss mornin' fer a yarner tew, an I hev promist ter cum in fer bitter skwit Ole Yeer's Nite anorl if theyll let me owter the Datty Duck for I git mer rown in.

Mynd how yer go tergather. Dunt drink tew much o' that cowld beer, and dunt scorf orl that grub inter yer at wun go. Jest yew be keerful yewre got suffin left for 1981. Weel hatter dew searme thing then, yer know ... thassit ... Dew yew keep a' troshin!

◇ *DATTY DUCK DING-DONG* ◇

*It was something of a surprise that Old Barney made it into
Radio Norfolk on Christmas Morning, 1980. He confessed to
being a bit under the weather after prolonged Christmas Eve
celebrations at the Datty Duck, with the regulars in full cry,
singing and supping. Even so, the rural show must go on – even
on Christmas Day.*

Mornin' ter orl on yer. Heyyer opened orl yer presence yit?
Thass marvlus wot they giyyer, ent it . . . lyke twetty fags when
yer dunt smook an' a raffell tickut fer last munths dror. Yew
shunt be ungreartful, I know, but wot the hell am I spoozed
ter dew wi' a new dickshunry an' a setter flyin dux ter stick
crors the worl?

Leest I dint git nunner that linjery stuff or arter shearve wot
mearke yer stink nyce arter yewre cleered the pigs owt.
Crearze me, that stuff, an I dunt wont blooks lookin' at me orl
funny, dewer?

Enny how, Ire gotter bitterer skullearke arter larst nites
dew down the Datty Duck. Thass allus good larf Chrismuss
Eve, but this wuz bit speshal an' thass no wadderer lye.
Trubbel wuz they started afore seven, an hossed few pynts
inter Cloddy so heed play the pianner an' git us orler singin.
Cloddy ent shy, but that took few jars for heed sorter joyn in
an' hev a bitter skwit. His mawther wuz theer, an she keep a'
garpin ter see he dint zakkly show hisself up. Then she cleered
orf bowt harpast nyne when he rowled his trowsers up an'
started a Conger owter the lavertry an back. Rekun heez
gittin' rite clipper the lug this mornin. Well, arter sheed gon
inner huff, Cloddy got ole Lilly Clayton ter show bitter leg an'
give us a song. She dew yorper bit an twist har ole dyall bowt,
an yew kin see har pashun killers when she giyyer bitterer
fling. Handy vew anorl! Rum mawther in har tyme, they say,
an sheer sin tew husbins orf. Shunt wotter be the thad. Sheez

They hossed few pynts inter Cloddy so heed play the pianner an' git us orl a' singin. Thass allus good larf Chrismuss Eve.

orrite when sheez hevvin good tyme an' blooks are bungin fer few drinks, but they rekun she hent harf gotter temper onner when thass tyme ter stop slewsin an' git hoom. We think Cloddy sor har orf the premises, an I hent sin him this mornin jest yit.

Darft thing bowt Chrismuss Eve down owr pub is way them wot dunt hevver yap wiyyer orl yeer start clackin an' arskin how yewre gittin on. Thass darft cors yew dunt know who the hell they are – an yer dunt see 'em gin till next year. Lanlord dunt ceer while heez stickin' munny itter the till, an' gittin' few free drinks owt onnit anorl.

Muster mearde fortewn larst nite if m' skullearkes ennything ter go by. "Are yer gorter hev wun, Barney?" they keep sayin, an yer dunt lyke ter disserpoynt em.

Gibby Painter an hislot wuz spoozed ter hevver taxi, but they wuz ser jewsed up they started walkin' for that got theer. Lilly wuz still a' gowin strong at chuckin-owt tyme, hollerin' when nowun wunt lissnun, an' arskin fer them Green Goddisses when bar wuz shut. Dunno bowt Green Goddisses; sink that took fyre injun ter gittar hoom. When she larf thass lyker syren gowin orf. Dunt git me rong. We arnt looder boozers in the willuj. Thass jest we lyke ter git in the festiv mood an' hcvver bitter skwit for we git down ter seryus bizness o' eetin an' hevvin a kip whyle telly's on. Thass nyce ter hevvcr breark, but thass no good sum onnem gowin back ter wak feelin' proppa beggard. Thass orrite fer the yung hellyuns. They kin stick it, an go owtfer nuther gutful sewns they git owter bed.

Ire gotter git down Datty Duck ter wish em orl the best. Then I'm gorter git m' dinner ... nyce fesant wot sumwun bort me larst week ter lettit hang, an bitter puddin ole gal next door sed she dint wont. Thatell dew me longer bottel or tew wot I searved up fer. If yer hearve yarselves, Oill hoss itter heer Ole Yeers Nite wi' moi Orlmunack fer 1981. Tiller dew, joy yarselves in moderearshun, say thankyer even if yer dunt git wotyer spected, an' mooster orl ... Dew yew keep a' troshin!

There was a big surprise in store for Radio Norfolk listeners on Old Year's Night, 1980. Old Barney duly arrived, but, for once, he hadn't come by bike. His cousin Horry acted as chauffeur, and also joined forces with the rural correspondent to size up prospects for the coming twelve months. Some of their forecasts weren't too wide of the mark ...

Evenin' ter orl on yer. Thass whooly nyce ter hevver yap wiyyer Ole Yeer's Nite, an' I hoop yer arnt gittin tew mucher that ole jews inter yer so yew hevver proppa skullearke ter start 1981 with.

Ire binner thinkin bowt larst twalv munth, an that dunt add up ter lot, dew it? So me an' m' cussin Horry hev hossed itter heer ter giyyer few sujjestyuns wot mite be gowin on from tomorrer. Yew mite say thass looder skwit, but weer got owr lugs ter the grownd, me an' Horry.

Fast thing we rekun's a' cummin up is a weddin in the willuj. Ole Cloddy's gorter tye the not an' git hitched ter that mawther wot heer binner bringin down the Datty Duck. Wuh, theerl be darnsin, drinkin, larfin an hell know wot if he desyde ter mearke honist wommun onner. Oid lyke ter see 'em on thar hunnycoom wi' Cloddy weartin on har hand an' foot.

Enny how, thass gooder Horry ter bring me down heer ternite. He carnt drink whyle heez dryvin, but I hent got ner scewses fer tannin down jarrer tew. Nyce pynter myld, thated go downer treet rite now. Horry ... woddyor cristul borl say, an dunt yew be datty lyke wot yew are when yew go ter them footbawl gearmes ...
HORRY – "Spooz fast thing'll be Prinse Charles dewin a' Cloddy an gittin' splyced. That Dianner Spenser mawther, sheel be the wun. An that wunt sprize me if Dick Condor dint try ter git the resepshun at the Theetre Royle."

BARNEY – "I did heer he wuz orf ter joyn Crossroods, wi' Benny tearkin over the Theetre. Noffin wunt sprize me ennymoor – not arter they put that 'Oh Grasscutter' on the stearj few munth back."

HORRY – "Dunno bowt puttin on. Moor lyke tearkin orf, wunt it? That show woss on now must cum as a rare ole chearnj fer Benny. Heez wakkin wi' peeple wot kin member thar lynes!"

BARNEY – "Oim gorer look forrad ter Febbry now, an I say well be lucky if we arnt bunged up wi' snow. Thass bin tew mild fer my lykin upter now. Thatull be orrite if Cownty Cownsil kin git sum grit an' sum shuvels. Thass pitty them cuts dunt meen they kin shut harf the roods an' buy helikopter."

HORRY – "Thass allus windy in March, entit? So Oim gorter keep orf them pickled unyuns an be moor soshubel. Spooz Norridge'll still be in the F.A. Cup ber then, and weel orl be yappin' bowt gorn ter Webbley agin. Thass orrite longers they dunt hoss itter Sekund Dervision anorl."

BARNEY – "Thyell be orrite vydin they git back ter tew wingers."

HORRY – "Wot wun eech syde? Orl dipend if that Joustin Fashanew stay at Carrer Rood. Thyere gotter keep feedin him them hy borls."

BARNEY – "Mearke it bit hard ter swoller. Cood be good summer fer chearnj. I wotter suntann this yeer – notter nyce rust. Theyere orgnizin trip ter Yarmuff from Datty Duck Darts Club, an thatell be treet if we kin keep em soober for we git theer."

HORRY – "Them hostritches shood be owt sewn if that Ronuld Raygun dunt go an' tiddel it up. Jimma Carter, heez gorter rite his memwahs, an Robin Day'll probbly cum Pryme Minster."

BARNEY – "No, my munny's on Dearvid Frorst. He cum from rown heer, yer know, an heer gotter good skull on them showlders.

HORRY – "Barnard Matthews orter mearke nuther millyun if he keep sayin' 'bewtiful' on thole telly. They say weer sorft in theez parts, but he know wot heez up tew."

BARNEY – "Spooz weer gotter say Reardyo Norfik mite git

better. They lyke it in our willuj, dunt ther? Thass lokul news,
they say, an they play rekuds fer peeple yer know. But theyll
hatter git ridder that Jimmy Yung; he clack on suffin wicket,
an he hent menshund Fearknhum ner Deerham yit."
HORRY – "Less hoss forrard ter the Ortum, an I kin see
Barbra Woodhowse gittin' distemper an' Basil Brush gowin
on the mowlt."
BARNEY – "Yeh, an I kin see that Anjeler Rippen gowin fer
lecktrekushion lessuns ter git fer that brekfust tellerwishun
job."
HORRY – "That ent eezy ter dew much fourcarstin cearse
they drop fewer them Crewd Missyles orl over the shop whyle
weer hevvin kip wun nite."
BARNEY – "That unt happin in 1981. Things are gorter git
better if we keep owr peckers up an dunt tearke tew much
notyce o' orl tham polertishuns. Let 'em slarver on. We know
wot weer gotter dew. Keep smylin, keep senser perporshun.
Moost o' orl, look 1981 streart in the oiy. Happer New Yeer
... an' ... Dew yew keep a' troshin!"

It's obvious by now that the local pub plays a major role in the lives of Old Barney and his rural cohorts. And in his mardle of January 3rd, 1981, the old boy has a few sharp words about the way pubs are changing. "A pub is a pub, not a supermarket or an amusement arcade" – that's the key message as a New Year dawns.

Mornin' ter orl on yer. They say heyyer hadder nyce Chrismuss, dunt ther? Yew say yis, cors yewre had pletty o' grub, lotter booz an' bitterer gut earke ter proov it. Then they say, dew yew hev a happer New Yeer, assif thass an order. They gorp atyer lyke yewre gon barmy when yew tell 'em that ent lykely ter git much betta longus peeple are still bowt ter muck things up.

Trubbel is theer ent nuff onnem who hev good larf when things ent tew sharp. Leest they mearke un effut down Datty Duck, an we wuz necrly bustin arselves thuther nite when orl onnem wuz arsked fer thar New Yeer reverlushiins. Cloddy gotter bitter stick cors they rekun heel be gittin marryed for long. But he wuz fast ter cum owt wi' suffin sensibul. He say heez gorter git few moor in darrin 1981. Coont git ner less, cood he? Heez allus larst up ter the bar arter crickut, an that meen he dunt gitter drink atorl if the boys he' lorst an heer give wun or tew dodjy dercishuns ginst 'em.

Gibby, wot mearke harfer myld larst whool nite, say heez gorter go hoom bit arlier so he ent ser tyred in the mornins. Spooz heel be hevvin a qworter o' pynt from now on. Misrubel ole bugger ... when he say heez gowin fer a rown, we allus think he meen heez orf ter play golf longer the nobs.

Lanlord did say he wuz gorter shut shop bit sewner cors weer gittin bad reputearshun fer hangin bowt arter cloosin' tyme. But weer torked 'im owter that wun. Heer gotter mearke livin, hetee, an weer gotter hev sumwheer ter go when thass rearnin an theer ent noffin on the telly. Iyre sed afore summer the pubs rown heer hev gon rite orf wi' orl them spearse vearders an skwit lyke that. Peeple hent got tymer ner moor ter yap ter eech uther when theyre twiddlin wi' nobs an crunshin itter glaxies when they cum hossin down. Theyere gittin evrything from astroyds ter hemmeroyds on them bloomin mershines, but we dunt let 'em git in the wayer evrything at Datty Duck. Yew kin allus jog sumwuns elber when theyere consentratin. Yewre orrite longers yer dunt git pooker the lug.

Iyd lyke ter see pubs mearke sartan chearnjes fer the betta in 1981. They cood mearke the beer cheeper forra start, an hev a rewl that yewre gotter hev reel fyre stedder wunner them imitearshun jobs wot dunt chuck owt ner smook.

Thass orl plastik, entit? Pertend this, an' pertend that. Summer the clynts wot sarve yer looks if theyere lorst a shillin' an' fownd a tanner. Rekun theyere a' dewin yew a fearvur sellin beer at harfer kwid a pynt. Git on yer wick. Then they tellyer orf fer hevvin a song on a Satterday nite. Cor blarst, we ewsed ter rearse thole roof few yeer back, an' orl onnem did a tann. Weer orl bit syted abowt this heer brekfust tellerwishun, cors thatell be on tyme we git hoom from the pub. Thass nyce ter know woss gowin on in the wald for yer hevver cupper tee an git down the lotmint. They did hevver telly down the pub, moosly fer them wot wotted ter see footbawl but wotter stay indors. Thass suffin else wot crearze yer when yewre tryin ter joy yarself ... and weer putter ban onnit sept fer Coronearshuns an' nashnul marjun-sies, lyke a poor harvist or the Budjit stickin beer pryces up agin. I know we carnt go back ter thole daze – and they wunt allus as good as sum onnem rekun – but a pub isser pub, that ent supermarkit or mewsement arkade. Yew go forrer clack an' a jar. An thass owr reverlushin down the Datty Duck. Ter keep it a reel pub fer peeple wot know howter ewse it. Oim gorter tearke m' fast proppa hollerday fer over thatty yeer anorl in 1981. Arnt gowin hykin or searlin or noffin posh lyke that. I fanser wunner them crewses on a gret big lyner, an a bit farther 'n Scrooby Sans anorl. Yew nivver know, I cood finush up lyke Cloddy wi' nyce bitter stuff ter cleen m' shews an git mer grub riddy. Im a gowin threw them broochers ter git few idears, but I dunt spooz orl them mawthers are kwite's smart an' shearply lyke they mearke owt. Still, thass suffin ter keep me gowin' darrin the winter. Iyre got bitter diggin ter dew terday. If yewre gorter footborl at Carrer Rood, givvem a holler fer me ter help em win.

Dunt git tew downharted, but hevver go if yar pub's gowin orl plastik. Dewit wi' reel smyle, thow, an keep that gowin way itter the New Yeer. Orl the best. Keep tewned in. Pay fer yer rown, an dunt yew fergit … Dew yew keep a' troshin!

When thass gowin full pelt, mud go hossin up itter thair, onter yer chops, rown yer lugs and upter the seelin if yer arnt ceerful.

The New Year fires many people with new enthusiasms – and Old Barney is no exception. He and Cloddy decide to put some of their spare time to good use at local evening classes, although one suspects it won't be too long before they're back drawing pictures with words down the pub. Still, it's good to find them taking advantage of educational facilities, and their progress is reported on January 10th, 1981.

Mornin' ter orl on yer. Oim tryin' ter git mesself edeucearted a bit, so me an' Cloddy hebbin ter them new evenin' clarsses in the willuj horl. We hossed threwer lister things yew kin larn in yar speer tyme.

I wuz thinkin bowt yoggart clarses, but Cloddy say orl yer dew is lay onyer back an' spraddel yer legs buvyer hid. Spoozed ter be good fer yer brearn, but orl that dew is mearke yer dizzy. Cloddy, he know cors he hedder go wun nite in the Datty Duck arter heed hadder few. So we crorsed that wun orf, an went fer suffin bit moor sensibul at owr tymer lyfe.

Cloddy's gittin stuck itter woodwak so he kin mearke suffin fer the howse when him an' his mawther settel down. Heer started orridy on a tearbel fer the frunt room. Daft fewl left room fer nyne legs, dittee, so he hatter start agin.

Oim hevvin' go at pottry. Thass bit messy an' helluva job ter stop thole wheel when yer whantew. When thass gowin full pelt, mud go hossin up itter thair, onter yer chops, rown yer lugs an upter the seelin if yer arnt ceerful.

Weer got that Miss Spinx larnin onnus, an she say thet ent tew hard ter git the hang onnit. She showed us sum zampels, bitser jugs an' jars wot the Roomans ewsed ter hev on thar mentel peeses. When we towld em down the pub wot we wuz up tew, they orl larfed an corled us cuppel o' panzys. Then they fown owt summer owr clarsses clash wi' darts an' crib. Still, theers moor ter lyfe 'n' chuckin arrers an' shufflin cards an' metchstiks, ent ther? Theers helluva choyse fer them wot watter nite orf from the pub, an' I wunt be sprized if they dunt go rearly well how peepel h' got Chrismuss an orl that lot owter thar sistems.

Nuther thing theyere got gowin in theez heer clarsses is a short storey compertishun. Yewre gotter put targether yarn bowt suffin' streanj wot happent ter yew but yer carnt splearn it. Yew know, that put the wund up onyer, but thass gotter be trew.

Cloddy an' me, we dew hev few problims when that cum ter spellin. We wunt tew sharp at skool, but weer hevvin a go. Cloddy say he sor a goost wun nite neer the chatchyard. That wuz a crors twin a dorg an' a donkey, he say. We say he wuz harf cut, but he sweer blyn thass trew. We giv 'im tinner Chum an' bunsher carrets cearse he cum crors this annermal again, but he unt be put orf. That wuz wunner them apperishuns, he say.

I dunt bleeve in goosts, but I ent tew trucked up wi' the dark. My yarns gorter be bowt trew speryense wot I had on the farm sevrul yeer go when I wuz wakkin fer ole Tom Clippesby. That wuz snowin an' blowin, an that wuz whooly pitch black when I cum crors the back medder afore much onnit hed settled. Theer wuz helluva cermoshun in the hidje, and I dint lyke it wun littel bit.

I cood heer this heer thing, but theer wunt noffin ter see till I wuz jest bowt ter tannrown an git owt onnit. Then theer wuzzer grunt, an this rum ole blook cum charjin owter the dark wi' his ole hat in th' eer an' his gearters flyin bowt. He wuzzer tramp, an heed tiddled over on his way ter the barn ferrer nite's kip. He looktsif he wuz gorter run me threw, so I cleered orf pritty sharpish – an' I nivver did know if he hadder good kip. An I dint see ner moore onnim neether.

I orftin situn wunder wot happent ter him anorl them uther tramps wot ewsed ter be bowt. Still, thass long whyle ergo, but thatell mearke good yarn, oontit?

I shall hetter be orf cors Iyre gossum hoomwak ter dew, pottrin' bowt indors, I rekun. See yer next week fer nuther little natter. Mynd how yer go, speshslly if yer git the wind up eezy, an I hoop I dunt see yer in the wakhowse. Yew oont git theer if yer lissun ter wot I tellyer ... Dew yew keep a' troshin!

The village cricket club is a constant source of news and intrigue, on and off the field. In the middle of winter, the club's annual meeting fashions dreams of long, hot afternoons in the summer sun – and a quick dash to the bar for refreshment. A typical rural picture drawn on January 24th, 1981.

Mornin' ter orl on yer. Me an' Cloddy are gittin on orrite down them evenin' clarsses, but we hedder nite orf this week ter go ter thannyerl meetin o' the crickut club. They say Cloddy's mawther unt lettim owt ter umpyre ser much next seezun, but he say theer shunt be ner reel problims. We shall hatter weart an' see, sharnt we?

Summer the gals wot dew the tees say they carnt dewit no moor cors weer runnin owter cups an' pleartes. Moost onnem wuz hulled crors the villyun larst yeer when theer wuz barney bowt desishern wot Bilko Butterfield med. He giv wunner owr blooks owt when he wunt lookin' cors he rekun that wuz unjentulmenly konduck ter clobber the wickutkeepa rown the lug wi' his bat. The blook say that wuz axidunt, an' when wickutkeepa cum rown he dint henner complearnts. Still, Bilko stuckter his guns, an' orl hell let lewse when they started argrin at teetyme. They wuz chuckin stuff orl over the shop, an thass why we hent gotter lotter crockry ter speer.

Weel hatter hev bring an' by searle ter rearse sum munny for long, an' then weel see if them theer mawthers'll cum an' git owr grub riddy as ewsual.

Sum onnem wotter go inter this heer leeg crickut cors we hent got mennyer th'old fixtyers left. But we vooted ter stay as we wuz, an' jest enter evernin nokowt cups. Thass rear job ter git proppa teem owt arter tee, thow, so we mite hatter giv sumwun a workover if we git ser far an thass harvist tyme. Weer got new captun. Thass Cally Grant, who hent bin in the willuj long. He kin rite ferra start, an he ent tew bad at chukin onnem down for few ovas anorl. Heer played big crickut Lunnun way or suffin, but he hent gotter lotter swank. He git his rownd in regglar, an' I think thass why moost onnem stuck up thar hans. That wuz intrestin, thow, ter notise he dint bung fer mutch arter vootin wuz over. He ent sorft, I kin tellyer. We hent got tew menny yungsters in th' syde thees daze. Harf onnem dunt watter know when they kin cleer orf ter them disothews an' big pubs up the sity. We wuz tryin ter wak owt averij earje o' the teem arter the meetin – not cowntin me an' Cloddy – an' thass bowt thatty fyve an a harf. Thass hosin onner bit, ent it? Weer gotter cuppel boys wotter keen, but fewtyer dunt look tew sharp.

Weer gorter hev annyerl dinner lyke we dew evry yeer at the Datty Duck. Thass bin fixt fer Febbry longers that dunt clash wi' darts nor crib. Theyere gotter nyce littel back rum fer the job, and they git the ceartrers in fer hot soop an' stuff lyke that. We dunt hevver lotter speechin, cors boys lyke ter git ter the bar sewns theyere got thar grub down onnem. Annyel meetin dint larst that long. Bowt twetty minnit an then orf ter the bar. I bunged fer my lot, but Cloddy sorter stood back an' wistled when that wuz dew fer him ter be popplar. Rekun sumwun orter hevver wad in his lug bowt that.

Oill hev nuther littel clack wiyyer next week. Dunt stan back when thass yar tann. Git em in! And dunt yew fergit … Dew yew keep a' troshin!

Many people regret the demise of the old-style village police-man, pedalling around the parish to keep an amiable eye on people and property. And there were some outstanding characters among them – like Sticky Stainrod. Perhaps he's best remembered for his confrontation with Cloddy Gates one night after closing time . . . the case came up on January 31st, 1981.

Mornin' ter orl on yer. Thasser rummin how peeple clack bowt diffrunt things, entit? An they dunt reely know wot theyre spoozed ter be on bowt anorl. Yew tearke owr pub, Datty Duck. Argrements blow up owter noffin in tikler, an' for yer know woss gowin on, theyere a' hollerin teech uther an intruptin suffin wicket. Thass best ter lettem spuffel on an git it orf thar chists – and then tellem thass looder ole skwit. Moost onnem larf an by yer a harf.

They wuz hevvin rite go thuther nite bowt loranorder. Sidderin that wuz neer harparst leven for theyd dun cors lanlord dint notyce the tyme, that wuz bitterer cheek. Heez lyke that . . . whyle yewr bungin an yappin, he keep doolin it owt. Still, thass betteran orl this "Cleer orf, weer dun" lark.

Enny how, this heer debearte bowt loranorder. Cloddy kep stickin his tewpeneth in. He got nicked few yeer back fer rydin his byke wiowt ner lites. He got fyned ten bob, but he dint hev his lysense dorsed. He dint henner prevyus convix-ions, thow fars I kin member he beggered orf sevrul tyme cors heed hed a skinful. Silly ole fewl, heer dun poochin anorl, yer know, but he say thass parter country lyfe an natrel thing ter dew. Rummin he wunt cort thow.

Thole pleesman wot we ewsed ter hev, Sticky Stainrod, they rekun he cood be brybed. Hent gotner proppa evdense fer that, but that seemed sorter funny he hed fesunt fer dinner moost Sundays. He ewsed ter git on wi' moost onnem in the

*He cooder hulled the book attim, cors he hent got ner brearkes, bell
wunt wakkin an wunner the mudguards wuz missin.*

willuj, an he hadder cuppel uther plearses ter look arter
anorl. That wunt eezy hossin down them roods on his ole
byke, a rear boonshearker. "Send fer Stainrod!" they ewsed
ter holler when they started scrappin down the pub onner
Satterday nite. Tyme he git theer, they wuz opnin fer Sunday
pynt.

That wuz Stainrod wot dun Cloddy wun nite fer hevin no
lites on his byke. He cooder hulled the book attim, cors he
hent got ner brearkes, bell wunt wakkin an' wunner the
mudguards wuz missin. Cloddy fort the cearse an' wotted ter
corl witneses. Then he chearnjed his plee ter gilty arter they
sed heed hatter pay ten bob. He lookt rite sorft, speshlly when
they rit a funny bit in the pearper.

"Wellnown lokul umpyre stumpt ber the lore!" that say,
an' Cloddy got pletty o frewt bowt that littel lot. He wunt lone
that day at cort. Sum blook wot left the willuj sewn arter wuz
up fer bein drunkandisordly. He say he wuz drunk fars he
could member, but he coonter bin disordly cors he fell over an
hadder kip in th' bar. Wot he dint say wuz how he brook
thatty glarsses an' cueppl o' custumers snowts afore he did
smack his own skull ginst the flor.

Cloddy rekun pleesman terday are allus garpin attim cors
heer gotter rekud. Yew put wun foot rong in this wald, he say,
and yer allus gotter bung forrit. Mynd yew, he dew hev lites
on his byke now, an they wak mooster the tyme anorl.

We dint tearker voot down Datty Duck cors nowun reely
know wot whool poynt onnit wuz. Rekun mesself that wuz
jest crarfty wayyer gittin few moor jars in arter tyme. Gibby
wuz oonly wun ter cleer orf for leven, an that wuz cors that
wuz his tann ter gittem in.

Parsunlly, I say the coppas dewer good job in differcult
sarcumstanses. They orl look ser yung thow, dunt ther,
flashin parst in them pander cars an smart hats? They say
yewre gittin on when the pleesmin look yung. That must
mearke me bowt earty tew.

Still, rekun Oill be bowt next week fer nuther littel mardle
wiyyer. Mynd how yer go. Keep yer lites brite on yer byke.
Keep on rite syder the lor, and the rood. And dunt yew fergit
… mornin' orl, and dew yew keep a' troshin!

◇ *THE THINGS WE SAY!* ◇

We all have our own quaint little expressions or catchphrases, and many country folk owe their nicknames to something they've said – and then repeated! Old Barney turns his thoughts to this fascinating area on February 7th, 1981, thinking out loud as usual.

Mornin' ter orl on yer. Woddyer rekun onnit so far? They crearze yer down the pub when they keeper cummin owt wi' that wun, cors yer allus git searme arnser, dunt yer? Iyre bin hossin over in m' mynd summer the things wee say moor owter habbit thun ennything else, an wee dunt realyse jest how sorft we sown.

Cloddy say ter me thuther day "Theers darnse nex' Fryday down the horl, are yer gorter cum?" I say yis, an' then that struck me as sorter darft. How the hell kinnyer go an cum at searme tyme? Mynd yew, Cloddy dunt know if heez cummin er gowin harf tyme sinse that mawther o' hiz started stoppin' him playin darts annal when he feel lyke it. He git rong if he dunt teller wheer heez gowin. Spooz thass tyme sumwun trydter sortim owt. Theers sum wot arnt marreyin' kynd – lyke me iffyer lyke – but I say Cloddy ackshewlly njoy bein towld orf lyke sum kid. When theyer larfin attim, heez bein notist anorl.

Gibby Painter, him wot dunt bung tew orftin less heez shuved upter the bar an awdered ter gittem in – he say sum rum things wot heer bin cummin owt wi' evva sinse I kin member. "Dumplins are riddy" he chunter bowt harpast ten moost nites for he cleer orf hoom. "Prycer spuds is wicket", thass nuther o' his regglar wuns. An he wuzzer sayin that when bloomin' things wuz cheep. Then he cumowter "Gotter muk rabbits owt" when we arsk wheer heez orf tew in the middle o' gearmer crib. Fars I know, he dunt lyke dumplins ner spuds, an Oim sartan he hent gotner rabbits. Thass jist habit, entit?

When I wuz at skool larnin, wunner the boys wot had pletty oyap – Slumpy Denver I think that wuz – he wuz allus gittin a dinger the lug fer sayin darft things. He ewsed ter arsk them mawthers sum rum things, but he hadder funny wayyer puttin it crors. "Less mearke merry in the medder" wuz his favrit, thow I carnt zakkly recorl ennywun beyin tearkin in ber thoffer. Gals thowt he wotted ter play rownders or suffin, but teecher put peard ter orl his skwit when she arsked him wot he reely ment. Slumpy went orl red, dittee, an say he dint know. That wuz suffin his big bruther cum owt with, an he wuz jest repeetin onnit. Rite, say teecher, yew kin repeet it few moor tyme, carnt yer. Lyke fyve hunred tyme in yar exersyse book for yew go hoom ternite. Slumpy dint aggreveart us wi' that wun no moor, but that dint stopim orlergather. Dunno wheer he is now. Went inter Army yeers ago an sorter dispeered.

He hadder mearte Jumpy Turner. Jumpy wunt his reel fast nearme, but he got stuck wi' it corser the way he ewsed ter jumpup an down when ennywun put suffin tew 'im. His brearn wuz jest the searme, orl over the shop. Dunt think ennywun gotter sensibul arnser owt onnim till he marryed Milly Johnson. Her bruther wuz coolman, but they orl mooved way.

Yew member sum peeple by things they ewsed ter say, duntyer? Like thole parsun we ewsed ter hev for the wor. The Revrind Potter. Nyce ole boy, but he wunt reely wiyyer. Heed yap on wiowt lissnun tew yer.

"Jerhoover will proovyde" he say wotever yer arsked him. Spooz that wuz afor yer cood git dool munny. An that ole gal at the shop wuz nuther ... "Heyyer got nuff kindlin?" she say whenyer went in fer tinner beenz or jarrer jam. Kids corl har Ole Mar Kindlin, but leest she hadder larf wiyyer. Thass cors she hed tyme, stedder bustin gut lyke they dew terday.

Wuh, Oid better stop ramblin on tew much bowt the parst, an git down the lotmint. Oill hev nuther little yarn wiyyer next week. Jest yew be ceerfull if yewre gorter mearke merry in the medder. Member wot happint ter Slumpy Denver. Mynd howyer go – and dunt fergit ... Dew yew keep a' troshin!

◇ *OLD CHAPEL'S SHUT NOW ...* ◇

You could be forgiven for thinking that the pub is the social hub of Old Barney's village! Well, he does mention the Datty Duck now and again. But he also has a soft spot for the old village chapel, sadly now closed, and on February 14th, 1981 – St. Valentine's Day – he provided a few more memories.

Mornin' ter orl on yer. Scewse me if Oimer blowiner bit, but I hadter hoss in heer on m'ole byke, an Ire gotter git mer win' back ... We dunt git ner yunger, dew wee?

When I wuz bit fitter, I coont harf belt long them country roods. Mynd yew, theer wunt ser menny theez moters an triklearted lorrys bowt, crunshin parst yer sif yer dunt hev ner rite ter be theer. Orl yer hatter look owt forrin them daze wuz cearshnul trakter chuggin long, an cows wot brook owter the medder. That wuz reel begger at milken tyme when they cum moochin crors the rood wi' sum ole boy plodden ahynd wi' a stick, tellin em ter git moovon. Dint tearker lotter notyce. Sum thins yer jest carnt hurry. Iyre allus ridder byke, and thass best way I knower gittin fresh earen exercyse anorl at searme tyme. Me anmer meartes ewsed ter packowr ruksax an cleer orf fer pikniks an aventers when we wuz kids in the hollerdays. Chearsin rabbuts down gravil pits ... an summer them yung bitser mawthers anorl. They ewsed ter dew bitter cookin on opin fyre, but theyere cleer orf hoom sewns that wuz dark. Us boys wunt sceered. Yew arnt if yewre brort up in the country. Yew know theers gorter be owels annat swoopin down in the nite, so that shunt put wind up onnyer, shood it?

Trew, we wuz bit cheeky sumtymes, but yew sewn gotter clowter the lug if yew went tew far. Thass them wot carnt tearker jook wot git moost frewt. Wun ole boy lived in owr willuj an he dint lyke kids, so we ewsed ter crearze him ber nokkin on his dor an runnin way fitter bust. Heed haller up the rood and shearke his ole fist, an, blarst, we dassent go back that way till we thowt heed gonter bed. Grumpy ole sod, heed cumplearn ter teechers so yew got rong when yer went backter skool, but they dint go lot onnim neether. Fergit his reel nearme. We corled 'im Ole Grumpy Guts. Darft thing wuz he left sum munny ter the chapil when he dyed. That wunt harfer sprize, but that helpt ter restoor the roof wot wuz leekin. We hatter goter chapil three tymer Sundy whyle mum wuz sortin the howse owt an' dad wuz hevvin dooze. Dint mynd tew much cors yer dint hatter lissun cearse they arsked kwestyuns arter. Summer the preechers med yer larf, hammrin the pulpet an showtin "Owrmen!" ter wearke yer orl up arter prayers. Sum onnem went on bowt Mooses 'n' Zeykiyel sif they knowed em parsunnly, an one ole boy allus pict "Rocker Earjes" fer wunnerhis hims. He hed helluva lowd voyce, yew cood hardler heer Mrs. Claymoor at thorgan, har ole feet pumpin upandown ter git sum sown owt onnit.

Annyvassray tyme wuz nyce, thow yew hed ter larner resitearshun an stanup an sayit when that wuz yar tann. I hent got mucherer memory fer vasses, so I wuz lowd ter reed sum onnit. My bruther wunt ner good atorl, so they lettim tearke colleckshun wot went twords owtin ter seesyde.

We hadder speshul preecher fer tha annyvassray, an mooster the willuj tann up ter heer kids in thar new clobber. Ole Chapil's shut now, lyke moost onnem rown heer. Thass pitty reely cors that did larn yer ter hearve yarself bit betta, even if we did giv ole Grumpy Guts suffin ter gitton with.

Wuh, Iyre nearler got mer win' back, an I better be gittin hoom fer m' dinner. Gotter nyce stew terday, so Oill hoss orf an gittit bubblin. Sewnser red orl mer Wallentyne cards Oill be back ter hev nuther littel yarn wiyyer. Mynd how yer go. Keep smylin. Be nyce ter eech uther, cors that dunt corst yer noffin. And dunt yew fergit … Dew yew keep a' troshin!